The
Cooperative Parish in
Nonmetropolitan Areas

The
Cooperative Parish in
Nonmetropolitan Areas

MARVIN T. JUDY

ABINGDON PRESS
NASHVILLE AND NEW YORK

THE COOPERATIVE PARISH IN NONMETROPOLITAN AREAS

Copyright © 1967 by Abingdon Press

Library of Congress Catalog Card Number: 67-22761

SET UP, PRINTED, AND BOUND BY THE PARTHENON PRESS, AT NASHVILLE, TENNESSEE, UNITED STATES OF AMERICA

To the laymen in the Harrison County Larger Parish, both living and dead, who were willing to experiment twenty years ago in a cooperative ministry and who have remained faithful in their witness, and to the late Reverend John W. Ward, Sr., and the late Bishop Ivan Lee Holt, who were instrumental in bringing into being the Harrison County Larger Parish

Preface

This volume stems from a continuing need for a more definitive statement on cooperative plans for the witness of the church in nonmetropolitan areas. With the rise of lay movements, church renewal, new forms of ministry, and the ecumenical movement, the opportunities for the work of the church in nonmetropolitan areas are legion. It is encouraging that within the past five years a new interest has been manifested in nonmetropolitan church planning in every major denomination in the United States, Canada, and England. Cooperative parishes of various types are being born, and experimentation in new forms of ministry is going on in numerous areas.

My interest in cooperative parishes began with my first appointment as a Methodist minister in 1933 when I accepted the Birch Tree Circuit in South Missouri. After nine years in that charge I served four years in St. Louis. In 1946 I was asked by denominational executives to consider the development of the Harrison County Larger Parish on the Missouri-Iowa border. The district superintendent, the late John W. Ward, Sr., saw the need for a cooperative parish and had stimulated the interest in it. The late Bishop Ivan Lee Holt, at that time resident bishop in Missouri, made the appointment and gave un-limited support.

Bishop Holt had placed Floyd V. Brower, as he was leaving the chaplaincy, in Harrison County to study the situation and to assist the people in establishing a parish. Mr. Brower was quite successful. He became the director of the Pemiscot County Larger Parish in the fall of 1946 and remained in that position until 1964 when he became a district superintendent. E. I. Webber went with me to the parish in 1946. Mr. Webber now is the director of the Nodaway County Larger Parish in Missouri and is quite effectively using a group of trained laymen as speakers in the three congregations of the parish. The first staff in the Harrison County Larger Parish consisted of David E. Fields, H. E. Marshall, Elmer Evans, N. R. Eveland, W. W. Miller, E. I. Webber, and myself.

While serving the parish, I made a systematic study of parish literature and sought counsel with as many church-men as possible. Included were the late C. M. McConnell, Rockwell Smith, Aaron Rapking, the late Dumont Clark, Herbert E. Stotts, Earl Brewer, James Sells, Glenn F. Sanford, the late Elliott L. Fisher, A. W. Martin, Ralph L. Woodward, and the late Lawrence M. Hepple. Most of these persons visited the parish.

During the latter part of the five years in the parish, I started work at Iowa State University of Science and Technology at Ames, Iowa, in the field of sociology. Ray E. Wakeley, Joseph B. Gittler, and George Beal, professors, had a profound influence on my understanding of social theory, leadership, and rural sociology. My dissertation was an analysis of the Kirksville District consisting of ten counties. The superintendent, Joseph W. Thompson, was very cooperative and established several larger parishes as the result of the study.

In 1957 I was invited to participate in a summer school on the rural community at Candler School of Theology, Emory University. For three weeks a group of thirty-five persons, all specialists in town and country ministry, examined, criticized, and helped me rewrite a manuscript on the larger parish and group ministry. I am indebted to all of those persons and especially to Earl Brewer, Ross Freeman, and James Sells for inviting me to the school.

In 1959 Abingdon Press published *The Larger Parish and Group Ministry*. Since that date some of the more radical changes in town and country areas have taken place. I was asked by Harold S. Huff and Clyde N. Rogers to revise and update the above volume in 1964. Writing and research schedules at that time, however, prohibited the undertaking, but I did write a small document, *Parish Development Aids*, which was published by Abingdon Press in 1964. That material has been incorporated into this volume.

In November, 1966, I was privileged to counsel with Dr. George Beal at Iowa State University concerning the writing of this book. I am indebted to him for a number of suggestions and permission to use some of his materials on leadership.

Research for the preparation for this book has been made possible by a liberal grant from the Interagency Committee on Research of The Methodist Church. I sincerely appreciate the confidence placed in me by my colleagues on that committee and their sense of value in regard to the church in nonmetropolitan areas. The grant has made it possible for me to travel extensively to visit with leaders in cooperative parishes, conduct extensive correspondence, and employ the necessary clerical help and a research assistant for bibliographical research.

I am indebted to more than forty denominational executives in every major denomination for their counsel and guidance in the preparation of the book. I have had personal interviews with more than half of this group and corresponded with the others. Harold S. Huff and Clyde N. Rogers have been especially helpful and encouraging as I have been rewriting. In addition, I have been in correspondence with many leaders of cooperative parishes. Some have gone to great length to describe in detail their parish, and I am grateful for this service. Then there are the parish staffs who have taken time to visit with me in person, show me around, and go into detail about their work. All of this research has given me a backdrop for writing and added a freshness to the work. It has also convinced me that cooperative parishes are far beyond the experimental stage and are here to stay.

One of the highlights of my research was an evening spent with thirty-five laymen in the Cainsville Charge of the Harrison County Larger Parish and their pastor, the Reverend Bernard L. Noordhoek. It had been, almost to the day, twenty years since my wife and I went to the parish in 1946, and fifteen years since we left it. We were thrilled with the continued progress and witness of the congregations. The parish as an organization has ceased to be, but the churches are strong. Though Harrison County has lost five thousand in population since 1940, the Methodist churches of the county have in their membership 20.2 percent of the total population.

A sincere word of thanks is expressed to Mrs. Susie

Banks, research secretary in the Center for Research and Planning, who has tended to questionnaire correspondence, the many things which go into the preparation of a manuscript, and the final typing of the manuscript for publication.

In 1934 I was united in marriage with Murlene Garrett. No profession places larger demands upon a wife than does the ministry. Our ministry together, however, has been one of exploration and discovery of new forms of ministry in town and country areas. It is difficult to know where ideas originate, and in our concepts of cooperative ministries this has been especially true since Murlene has read extensively in the fields of the Christian life and witness and has shared in every phase of creative ministry, prayer, and devotion.

This book is so much a part of our lives together as we have shared more than thirty years of ministry that it is impossible to express appreciation or give just credit. Our sons, Marvin Garrett and Dwight Henry, have shared the inconveniences of a rural parish and the demands which have been placed upon their parents in continued ministry. The family joins with me as co-workers in ministry hoping that this work may find a useful place in the witness to the Word in nonmetropolitan areas.

> Marvin T. Judy
> Perkins School of Theology
> Southern Methodist University
> Dallas, Texas

Contents

CHAPTER I

The Nature
of Nonmetropolitan Society

In the early days of the development of America, pioneer settlers moved across the nation forming a pattern of rural culture peculiar, in most respects, to the United States.[1] The pattern of homesteading was the family-sized farm.

European tradition, from which the pioneer had come, was that of village life with all families living in the village moving out daily to till the soil surrounding the village. Towns in Germany, central Europe, and England, even until this day, are not classified as rural or urban, but as industrial or agricultural. If the predominant means of making a living is that of employment in a factory, mill, or mine, the village is industrial. On the other hand, if the predominant means of livelihood is agriculture, the village is agricultural. The village can be a sizable town or small city even up to as much as ten thousand population.

LAND SETTLEMENT PATTERNS IN PIONEER AMERICA

After the first few years of colonial settlement in America, when it was necessary to build a barricaded shelter for protection from the Indians, the colonists began building their homes on the land they were to cultivate. This pattern was emphasized and encouraged with the opening up of new territory, and "squatter's rights" entitled an individual to become sole owner of the land on which he built his cabin. The Homestead Act of 1862 increased the emphasis upon land ownership and living upon the land one tilled, making it possible for an operator of a farm to become owner if he lived on the land for a stated time. "Possession is nine points of the law" became a slogan meaning if one was on the land, he had a nine-to-one chance of becoming owner of it.

As families settled on the land in the open country, there was a usual pattern of institutional development. First, they built their cabins; second, they built a school; third, they built a church. Someone with an enterprising ambition built a store which became a general merchandising institution selling anything from a spool of thread to a full set of harness.

The school, church, and store served an area geographically small—usually, as far as the church and school were concerned—not more than three to five miles in radius. The people living in this service area of the church and school were dependent upon one another in several ways: fellowship and social life, mutual aid in times of disaster and sickness, mutual assistance in busy farming seasons. Thus, there grew up a neighborhood symbolized in a name: Big Sandy, Bald Knob, Liberty, Bethel, Mt. Moriah, and a thousand other names.

Locality Group I: The Rural Neighborhood

Thus, the rural neighborhood was born. In the pioneer days of settling the nation, the neighborhood played a vital role. It was the center of elementary school activities. In it was the church—one or more congregations. In the neighborhood were to be found a general merchandise store, a blacksmith shop, and sometimes a medical doctor. The neighborhood was isolated due to poor roads and slow transportation. It was necessary for a church and school to be established within the neighborhood structure if the people of the area were to have educational and religious opportunities. A neighborhood was compelled to be self-sufficient in most respects. Only the merchant made his way, with any degree of regularity, out of the neighborhood for the purpose of replenishing his supply of goods.

In the intimacy of the neighborhood, children were born, reared, educated, nurtured in religious living, married, and found their place in the economy of the area and conformed to the mores of the group. The cemetery became a part of the neighborhood structure usually close to the one-room church.

Such neighborhoods, three to six miles in diameter, have become the romantic symbol of rural America. The little red schoolhouse has been the place where many of our American statesmen and leaders found their early training. Stories and novels have been written by the score about romantic pioneer America.

The rural neighborhood has been the subject of many studies by rural sociologists. Entire texts have been devoted to the study of rural society with primary emphasis upon the rural neighborhood. Among the many definitions the most common is: "A rural neighborhood consists of an area in which people neighbor together; that is, visit, borrow tools and equipment, trade work, and cooperate in various other ways." [2] The rural neighborhood is usually composed of ten to twenty families living closely enough to visit one another, developing a common bond of friendship. There may be one or more institutions in the rural neighborhood. This can be a church, elementary school, general store, or a combination of these. There may be no institutions, but merely a social unit built around fellowship of common interests.

The rural neighborhood is rapidly changing. Good roads, modern automobiles and trucks have made the agricultural town, or even the distant city, very close to the residents of the neighborhood. The general merchandise store has dwindled in business until no longer does it have an adequate trade to warrant operation. Thousands of such crossroads stores have ceased to be. It takes less time for the rural neighborhood family to drive five to fifteen miles to town than it did for their grandparents to go three miles for their trading.

The one-room country school all across America is rapidly becoming a memory. Good roads and the school bus have brought consolidation, forcing the children to go to the larger school in town or a new consolidated

18

school in a different neighborhood. Through state control of funds, consolidation has been forced upon many rural neighborhoods whether the people wanted it or not. General opinion, however, at this time, is that consolidation is worth what it costs in neighborhood morale by the compensation of a much better quality of education.

Neighborhood rural churches by the thousands have suffered a like fate to that of the stores and schools. It has been estimated that the Protestant churches of America have been closing two thousand rural churches a year since 1930. There is no question that many of these churches have served their period of usefulness, for they have been the source of Christian guidance through the decades. The primary difficulty has been that there has been no systematic procedure devised by denominational executives for the closing of a rural church. The usual pattern has been that the church continued to weaken until the few remaining members became so discouraged that they finally, with a sigh, just let the program of the church go.

Sometimes the closing of a rural church has led to the reviving of a village church. The leaders in the rural church simply move their membership to a town or village church. However, the larger group of people in the rural church have not aligned themselves with another church, and thus they are lost to the membership of the church and left without a church home. This pattern calls for some systematic method of neighborhood study to be made before a church closes or is consolidated with another church.

In spite of the thousands of rural neighborhood churches which have closed in recent years, there are still thousands of them in existence. In The Methodist Church alone, there are approximately fifteen thousand rural neighborhood churches. Lawrence Hepple, reporting to the National Convocation on the Church in Town and Country, October, 1956, on some findings from his four-year study of the rural church in Missouri, states:

Open country churches [rural neighborhood churches] were located an average of 3.8 miles from another open country church, and an average of 6.7 miles from a church of the same denomination. At the time of the survey there was approximately one open country church for every 16 square miles in rural Missouri. In other words, on the average there was a rural church within two miles from every farm family. These numerous small and part-time religious groups may be maintained for a period of time, but it is well for the church administrators to re-examine the number and location of rural churches in relation to the total program of their respective religious bodies.[3]

What is the future of the rural neighborhood? This is a question the rural sociologist is asking across America. In the early thirties the opinion prevailed that the rural neighborhood was rapidly ceasing to be. Such an attitude aided in public school consolidation. Nevertheless, in a few years the sociologist was saying that the rural neighborhood was persisting, it was going to remain, at least for a time, as a part of American culture. It was discovered that when the school went out of existence, when the church died, when the store was gone, informal groups sprang up. They were primarily for the purpose of fellowship and the desire of the individual for communication with friends of like mind. In more recent years there has been a re-emphasis upon the vanishing rural neighborhood. Sociologists are not agreed. It is possible that the rural neighborhood is ceasing to function as an organizational unit but that it will remain as a social unit. Some sociologists believe that it is a part of the rural culture the same as the family and plays a vital role in cultural development.

A comprehensive study of research, which had been done since 1921, and a reporting of new research on the rural neighborhood and community was published by John H. Kolb in 1959.

The dynamic character of rural society in the first half of the century is revealed, at least in some respects, by its changing group relationships. Increased facilities for communication and travel, great mobility of both country and city people, as well as the passing of the frontier generations, have all contributed to such changes. More recent country dwellers have chosen to maintain some of their own neighborhood groups, at the time they have combined with others to form larger town-country community groups.

Neighborhoods were the results of deliberate choice, specialized concerns, and organized relationships more usually than of kinship or nationality ties, of simply proximity of residence, of restrictiveness or topography, or of "just neighboring" which characterized many of them at the time of the earlier studies. Nevertheless, the general trend has been toward a decline in the number of neighborhoods but with a tendency toward stability and continuity on the part of those which do persist.[4]

Kolb has attempted to form an empirical basis on which can be judged the reasons for the persistence of a neighborhood or the disintegration of a neighborhood. Factors involved are school, church, some form of economic enterprise such as a store, factory, creamery, and so forth, and the desire of the people themselves for the neighborhood to continue. All of the above are important factors, and where two or more of the institutions exist, there is likely to be an identifiable neighborhood.

Social contacts of various kinds play an important role in neighborhood solidarity, but they also tend to form new relationships which reach across neighborhood boundaries. Saddle clubs, hunting clubs, dance clubs, school activities stemming from a consolidated school make for associational groups which are not necessarily neighborhood-centered but "interest-centered." This is an urban trend as is reflected in urban associational patterns which have little connection with residential patterns.

It has also been discovered that through overt efforts on the part of outside leaders in farm organizations, churches, political or business agencies, the neighborhood could be retained as a meaningful group.

A factor of major importance in present cultural trends is the increasing out-migration of urban dwellers to the countryside. Modern transportation has made it possible for many people to have their country dwelling and their city work too. Also the "second home" in the country within a one-hundred-mile radius of major cities is changing the complexion of the neighborhood. The centers of recreation on lake and stream are attracting thousands of urban dwellers back to the country. Kolb describes an area near Madison, Wisconsin, where a rural church burned and was rebuilt to fit the developing pattern of neighborhood settlement. He states:

Within this locality there are small farm families, part-time farmers, large farms with gentleman farmers as owners who are also commercial and professional people in the city, their resident renters, gardeners, artisans, clerical workers, a commercial orchard grower, and a church bishop. Families from the city come regularly to church services and to such local events as the Sunday afternoon horse races. Here is something different in group arrangements. Even the architecture of the new church is an announced symbol of this difference, a transitional type of community relations, neither rural or urban, neither urban or suburban, nor even metropolitan, but neopolitan, like the early commune, a new form for a very old kind of group association where nearly every element of population and variety of occupation in the general society is represented within the local community.[5]

There is an increasing body of literature emphasizing the importance of nature in personal and cultural development, and the primary group as the means of establishing and retaining value norms. The rural neighborhood has been a natural environment for family development, but with rapidly changing patterns of association it has the potential of disappearing in mass society. Architects are attempting to catch something of the beauty of nature in the greenery, living stream, and fountain in the midst of a sprawling shopping center. City planners are setting aside vast acreage for parks, and developers of new residential areas are attempting to preserve the natural beauty of trees, flowers, streams, and lakes. Nature is one thing, and the value of community life as has been associated with the rural neighborhood is another. However, persons in open country neighborhood churches can accept a new responsibility in the preservation of their church as a major factor in the expression of the gospel in the primary group relationship.

In the midst of such change stands the rural church. In spite of the thousands of these churches that have been closed, there are tens of thousands of them still open. In some areas of America today seventy percent of the Protestant congregation are in open country. Most of these churches are small. Many of the churches must share a minister with another congregation and do not know the value of a well-rounded program of church activity.

What will be the fate of the neighborhood church? The answer to this question depends upon the strategy of the Protestant church in town and country areas. Two general hypotheses can now be stated for serving people by the church in rural areas: (1) If the neighborhood church is needed as a unifying force in the rural neighborhood, the Christian community is duty bound to keep it there and provide an opportunity for a full program of church activity; (2) if the church is not needed as an institution within the neighborhood for a unifying force, then the people who reside there must be provided with ministerial leadership and a church in which they may express their religious devotion. This church will be in another neighborhood or community center. If the latter case is true, some means of drawing the people of the neighborhood together with people of the area in which the church is located must be discovered. It is possible that through a common trade center, consolidated schools, farm organizations, and church activities, the people will have built natural affinities with one another. The major tragedy of the declining and dying neighborhood church has been that large groups of people have been left without a church

24

tie of any kind. Neighborhood ties are so strong that there is no feeling of oneness with people of another neighborhood; yea, frequently feelings of animosity are felt between neighborhood groups preventing the affiliation with a church in another neighborhood.

LOCALITY GROUP II: THE RURAL COMMUNITY

The second cultural area in rural society is the rural community. The word "community" is being widely used by the theologian, philosopher, and sociologist. It is derived from the Latin *commūnis,* meaning fellowship or community of relations or feelings. In medieval Latin it was used in the sense of a body of fellows or fellow townsmen. MacIver, in an early attempt at defining community, said, "By community I mean any area of common life, village, or town, or district, or country, or even wider area. To deserve the name community, the area must be somehow distinguished from another area, the common life may have some characteristics of its own such that the frontiers of the area have some meaning." [6] Kenyon L. Butterfield in 1918 distinguished the community from the neighborhood:

I wish to emphasize one point strongly. We must not confuse "community" with "neighborhood." A neighborhood is simply a group of families living conveniently near together. The neighborhood can do a great many things, but it is not a community. A true community is a social group that is more or less self-sufficient. It is big enough to have its own center of interest—its trading center, its social center, its own church, its own school house, its own garage, its own library, and to possess such other institutions as the people of the community need. It is something more than a mere aggregation of families. There may be several neighborhoods in a community. A community is the smallest social unit that will hold together. . . . A community is a sort of individualized group of people. It is both the smallest and the largest number of people that can constitute a real social unit. It is a sort of family of families.[7]

Butterfield would have his reader recognize a distinct difference between neighborhood and community. *This is important in our study for an understanding of the problems related to the rural church.* Sociologists have come to think of the rural community as consisting of a central town or village surrounded by several rural neighborhoods. In the central town will be found a sufficient number of institutions, as Butterfield so ably states above, to supply the day-by-day needs of the villager and resident of the rural neighborhoods. Dwight Sanderson in 1920 stated: "A rural community consists of the people in a local area tributary to the center of their common interests. The community is the smallest geographical unit of organized association of the chief human activities." [8] This definition has been the basis of many research projects, and along with the methods of community delineation has come what is probably the most universally accepted definition of rural community: "A rural community consists of the social interaction of people and their institutions in the local area in which they live on dispersed farm-steads and in a hamlet or village which forms the center of their common interests." [9] With Sanderson's insights as the basis of community definition, a working statement of the meaning of community is presented for the sake of analysis: (1) People and/or institutions in social interaction; (2) A definable geographical area; (3) A psychic feeling among individuals which gives a feeling of "identity-with"; (4) An understood relationship which controls the mores of the community life; (5) A constellation of institutions and services rendered for the benefit of the people of the community.

A brief discussion of each of the above is presented.

1. *People and/or institutions in social interaction.* Within the community structure there must be mutual sharing of time, energy, social activities, and institutional life. Every rural community has in it the opportunity for people to come in contact with one another. Families mix together in church, school, and business organizations and are constantly having interaction either in cooperation or conflict. In short, people are thrown together in common everyday activities. Individuals are known in those relations that naturally evolve out of such associations.

2. *A definable geographical area.* The territory for intimate social interaction is naturally limited by geography. There is a limit to which people can travel for trade, institutional, and social life. A later chapter will deal with methods of determining the geographical community boundary. This is a vitally important factor in church administrative areas.

3. *A psychic feeling among individuals which gives a feeling of "identity-with."* The residents of a community quickly come to identify themselves with the community in which they reside. One can ask the question, "What is your community?" and an answer will be given, "Pleasant Valley" or "Centerville." There is a loyalty developed

in the mind of the resident. This is expressed in civic pride, support of school athletic groups, church, and community enterprises.

4. *An understood relationship which controls the mores of the community life.* Every community has personality. Customs are established which carry over from generation to generation. Many times customs are difficult to change and become detrimental to progress. Moral standards are established. Individuals who break out of such standards receive the condemnation of the group. One can observe the customs, beliefs, and attitudes of a rural community and type it in a single sentence.

5. *A constellation of institutions and services rendered for the benefit of the people of the community.* All people are in need of certain services to maintain normal existence. For instance, everyone must have a basic way of making a living, a means of educating his children, a means of worship and religious expression, social contacts and recreation, communication with others through the voice and written page, contact with a doctor and lawyer. Therefore, there are six services which the community will supply in part or all together: (1) economic; (2) educational; (3) religious; (4) social; (5) communicative; and (6) professional. Most of these needs are supplied through organized services rendered to people.

A brief analysis of each service is presented:

1. A community must offer its residents resources to make a living. There must be adequate job opportunities, a soil strong enough to support its owner or renter, or businesses or industries in which one can sell one's services. Without adequate economic resources, community structure soon disintegrates.

2. All people stand in need of education. Formalized education has been provided for in the development of an intricate program of public education. Community life consists of opportunities to educate children, youth, and adults. Through special programs of adult education, the chance for a continual development of the intellect should be provided.

3. Religious needs have been a part of every civilization since the beginning of the history of man. The community must provide through its institutions opportunities for worship and the expression of one's religious faith.

4. Social relationships are as deeply rooted in the human structure as religious desires. All people have the herd instinct. They want to associate with friends; they want to do things together during leisure hours. The community structure must consider this fact and provide opportunities for such association. Commercialized social and recreational activities have become a part of the American culture. The movie house, the park, swimming pool, and less desirable forms of commercialized recreation are a part of the community structure.

5. All communities must provide resources for communication of its people within the group. Transportation facilities must be adequate. Road systems in our modern culture are proving to be a decided pattern of rural community development. The telephone communication is an important function of community structure. With the breakdown of the rural telephone system since 1920 and the refusal of public utility companies to rebuild rural lines, the rural electrification cooperatives have moved into the area of building a strong communication

system among rural people. The weekly town newspaper has been a source of important rural community communication.

6. Professional services must be available for all people. There are legal matters which require the services of a lawyer, physical needs requiring the services of a doctor, religious needs requiring services of a minister. In the community structure these needs must be provided for. One of the difficulties facing the small rural community is the fact that professional people have refused to live among and serve rural people. This phenomenon is one of the deciding factors in the development of the enlarged community structure described below.

With the above definition of a rural community and the six types of services rendered by that community before the reader, it will be seen immediately that it is not possible for each rural community to have all of these services available. Therefore, to a certain extent, the number of services in a community determines the size of the community. Communities, then, are classified in various categories. According to Kolb and Brunner, there are five types of communities dependent upon the extent of the services provided to the constituent members of the community:[10]

1. *Single service community.* This is composed of people living in a village and open country with only one of the six services available. This is an elementary school, a church, a general store. Seldom does such a community consist of more than two hundred people in the village center.

2. *Limited service type community.* More than one service, but not all six, are offered and made available

in the community structure. It is a village (and the territory surrounding it) of two hundred to five hundred inhabitants. Approximately eighty percent of the trade of such a community center is drawn from the area around the central village.

3. *Semicomplete service type community.* The central village or town of five hundred to one thousand inhabitants offers most of the six major services, but not necessarily all. Approximately seventy-five percent of the trade in the central town is drawn from the surrounding area.

4. *The complete, partially specialized service type community.* The central town is composed of one thousand to five thousand inhabitants. It offers to its residents all six services and may offer some specialized services, such as a small hospital. It may be the countyseat town with several lawyers. There may be small factories, advanced opportunities for learning, recreational facilities, and so forth. Approximately fifty percent of the trade of the town is drawn from the surrounding community rural area.

5. *The urban or highly specialized service community.* All six services are offered in the community center, plus fields of specialization in all areas.

Karl A. Fox and T. Krishna Kumar hold to a concept which relates the size of a town or city to the economic services supplied. The following classifications are given:

First, there is the *full convenience center,* typically of 1,000 to 2,500 population and from $1,000,000 to $5,000,000 annual volume of retail sales. Second, there is the *partial shopping center* of 2,500 to 5,000 population and about $5,000,000 to $10,000,000 of retail sales. A good many of the small- and medium-sized countyseat towns in Iowa would fall in this category. Third, there is the *complete shopping center,* typically of more than 5,000 and less than 25,000 population with $10,000,000 to $40,000,000 of retail sales.[11]

The services rendered in the community center become the means of drawing the boundary lines of the community outreach. This is discussed more fully in Chapter VII. It is sufficient to state that the rural community is composed of a geographic area with one village or town surrounded by several rural neighborhoods. The central town is the center of common activities, from which the people of the area derive for the most part their primary or day-by-day services.

In the structure of modern rural life, the community is vitally important as a social unit. The development of a strategy for a church in the community setting, considering natural affinities, is one of the tasks of the church. It is possible, for instance, to develop a program within a community structure that could not be developed between two communities. To attempt a program of closely integrated work in two communities is to invite defeat. Churches attached together for a consolidation, extended ministry, enlarged charge, yoked field, or federated church should be in the same community for harmony. There is frequently a high degree of jealousy and competition between contiguous rural communities. Athletic contests, the competition for business, competition for receiving county or state aid for maintaining public schools or roads —all lead to friction between communities. Such friction inevitably creeps into the church and can spell defeat in cooperative programs. *A clear comprehension of the neigh-*

borhood and community concept is one of the first essentials for the development of a strong program of the church in town and country areas.

LOCALITY GROUP III: THE ENLARGED COMMUNITY

The third sociological unit in rural society is the enlarged community. To date, there has been little scientific research on the enlarged community comparable to that for the rural neighborhood and community. This is, no doubt, because it is a rather recent development and has come with the consolidation of schools and good highways. An enlarged community consists of two or more rural communities bound together in a natural or political area, with a dominant town in which all communities have a common interest. This is frequently synonymous with a county or part of a county. Figure 1 maps the typical rural neighborhood, rural community, and enlarged community.

There are many things which draw rural people together within the county structure. All people have the same county government. Services of the county agricultural agencies are at the command of all people in the county. School supervision, even to a county school board, is established on a wider perspective than the local community. Consolidation of high schools has brought the mind of the people to think beyond their local area. There are some sociologists who now feel the rural county —that is, a county with the central town no larger than twenty-five hundred people—is becoming more "community-like." In other words, the qualities of community as described above are applicable to the entire county.

Approximately one half of the counties in the United States, or fifteen hundred, fall in this classification.

There are hundreds of counties in the nation which have towns of more than twenty-five hundred population which are still rural in their outlook. Many counties have towns of five thousand, ten thousand, or even twenty thousand which are dependent primarily upon the agricultural operations in the surrounding area for their major economic activities. These counties, though not rural in the technical sense as defined by the United States census, are rural in outlook. Enlarged communities are formed around such towns and become important administrative units for the church.

For all practical purposes in rural church administration, the county serves as the basis of study. Population data, information on housing, agriculture, business, and industry can be secured on the county basis. There are areas of cooperation in church work by all churches in the county which cannot be accomplished by churches in adjoining counties. One must always be mindful of the rural community structure within a county, however, and recognize there are limitations to what can be done beyond the rural community. In subsequent chapters, organizational procedures within the enlarged community area will be discussed. With approximately one half of the counties in the United States classified as rural, one can readily see how important this unit is in the structure of nonmetropolitan America.

Natural barriers, such as rivers, lakes, mountains, and forests, may divide a county into two or more enlarged community groups. Another factor may be the existence of two towns of almost the same size. If there is, for example, a town of two thousand population which is the county seat and a town of twenty-five hundred which is not the county seat, there most likely will be much friction between them. This may make it impossible for the two towns to work together.

Other counties may have a larger town, up to ten thousand population, and a subordinate town of twenty-five hundred. It is possible that an enlarged community would

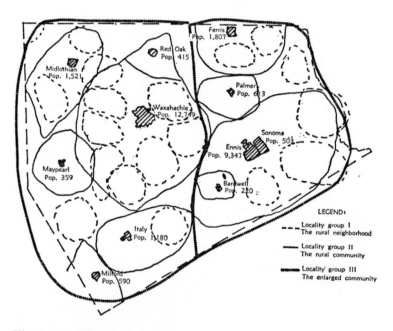

Figure 1. Ellis County, Texas. The three meaningful sociological units, locality group I, rural neighborhood; locality group II, rural community; and locality group III, enlarged community, are illustrated in the above map of Ellis County, Texas. Major delineation was done on the basis of traffic-flow map.

be around each of these towns or one of them, not including the other. Therefore, it may be said that the enlarged community consists of one dominant town with one or more subdominant towns and their surrounding rural neighborhoods, bound together by natural, political, or trade affinities.

LOCALITY GROUP IV: THE FUNCTIONAL ECONOMIC AREA

In recent years there has emerged a fourth meaningful locality group in nonmetropolitan areas, the Functional Economic Area (hereafter referred to as FEA). Some of the most extensive work on the FEA has been done by Karl A. Fox in the department of economics at Iowa State University of Science and Technology and his colleagues in economics and sociology. Fox has used the old Charles J. Galpin concept of the trade area community of 1911–1913 which was published in a bulletin, "The Social Anatomy of an Agricultural Community," [12] and has applied it to the contemporary scene with good roads and rapid automobile transportation. Galpin held that a town would draw persons in the countryside to it for various types of trade and services. If within a county there were several towns, each would have around it a trade area which would become a "community." Due to slow transportation and poor roads in 1913, the trade area was limited to approximately a one-hour travel distance, or a radius of approximately five miles. Using the state of Iowa for research, Fox has shown how there are major cities which serve an economic area of an approximate fifty-mile radius, or one-hour travel time on good roads by automobile. A rectangle is used rather than a circle be-

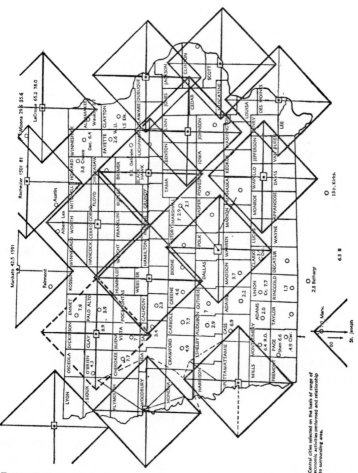

From Karl A. Fox and T. Krishna Kumar, "The Functional Economic Area: Delineation and Implications for Economic Analysis and Policy," Department of Economics, Iowa State University, Ames, Iowa. March 20, 1965. Mimeographed.

Figure 2. The Functional Economic Areas of the State of Iowa.

cause roads are laid out on section lines rather than diagonally. In other words, one would have to travel so many miles east or west and so many miles north or south to reach the city. Fox draws the conclusion, then, that the entire state of Iowa could be compared with Galpin's Walworth County, and the seventeen Functional Economic Areas of the state of Iowa and its bordering cities in the neighboring states could be compared with the ten trade area communities of Walworth County. (See Figure 2.)

The FEA then becomes the center for major marketing, trade, specialized services, higher education, and employment. Fox contends that people will travel up to fifty miles in one direction for such services.

For the purposes of church administration the FEA can become a meaningful planning area for denominational and interdenominational work. At this time it is too large an area to think of for cooperative parishes, but it has significant meaning in regard to a base to start from for regional church planning. Some church planners envision the FEA as the basic unit in the future for the ecumenical church in nonmetropolitan areas.

COMMUNITY AS A SOCIAL SYSTEM

The term "locality group" has been used in this chapter because it refers to a specific geographic form or a territory which can be defined. For analytical and administrative purposes the descriptions are viable and meaningful. However, a trade area community (locality group II) or an enlarged community (locality group III) do not necessarily mean that there is a meaningful "community" in the sense of common understanding and fellowship. Writers in the field of community have attempted to formulate concepts of community which are not geographically limited, but which will include persons who are of like-mind and like-interests.

Among other theories which have emerged is that of the community as a social system. Charles P. and Zona K. Loomis hold that various social theories in regard to human relations have been built around nine major elements of interaction:

> From among these aspects those that are considered elements are (1) belief (knowledge); (2) sentiment; (3) end, goal, or objective; (4) norm; (5) status-role (position); (6) rank; (7) power; (8) sanction; and (9) facility. At any given moment in time the structure of a given social system may be described and analyzed in terms of these elements.[13]

As one thinks of community as a social system, Loomis' concepts can serve for analytical purposes:

1. *Belief* (knowledge). A belief is centered around what one holds as ultimate truth, or that which is of vital importance. Belief may carry with it a sense of destiny or ultimate reality.

2. *Sentiment* conveys the concept of "how one feels about it." Values are placed upon certain things, loyalties created and understood.

3. *End, goal,* or *objective* indicates the concepts of persons involved as to what they consider to be their purpose in life along with other persons. As common goals or objectives arise, a sense of oneness with others is developed.

4. *Norms* are established by every group of people.

39

They are inherited from a preceding culture, altered by individual desires, fused with other cultures, but usually fairly well understood by a body of people of like-mind.

5. *Status-role* (position) indicates what is held by the body of people to be symbols of attainment with a hierarchy of values.

6. *Rank* implies a hierarchy of positions within a culture which are assigned to leaders and followers within the society.

7. *Power* refers to authority which is invested in persons or the system for decision-making, action, enforcement of sanctions, and bringing into being that which is best for the group.

8. *Sanctions* are the self-imposed disciplines of a body of people for control of the persons within the group. Sanction implies rewards for certain achievements and disciplines for infraction of the understood standards of the group.

9. *Facility* implies the process by which the group is able to attain its ends, goals, and objectives and to operate as a social system. It may imply government, a constitution, authority, leadership, understood roles, and positions.

From the brief analysis above, it can be observed that wherever the nine criteria exist, there exists a social system. It does not limit the social system to a geographic location, though it does not exclude such from the definition.

Within the geographic community (locality group II), there may be a number of subsystems operating. Each denomination will be a social system within itself. The public school becomes a social system. Fraternal organizations become social systems. Usually, however, there are enough cohesive elements within the geographic community to find the "makings" of a social system.

As cooperative church programs are planned, natural associational groups need to be discovered. Such groups can become the foundation for cooperative strategies in church administration.[14]

Trends in Nonmetropolitan America Affecting the Church in the Small City, Town, and Country

In the society in which we find ourselves, we are aware that we are the recipients of all that has gone into the past to develop that which is commonly known as our culture. We are the products of it and at the same time the creators of an ever-changing new culture to emerge in a new society which shall follow us. We live in a society which is not static but dynamic. A dynamic society is one that is changing. Some changes as far as the moral and cultural good of mankind is concerned are good; some are bad. Only the future can tell the final outcome of the effects of our living of the day. Changes are inevitable in a growing society, and they always bring about a tension between the new and the old. Changes call for a rethinking of the old, a reevaluation of the old, a preservation through concerted effort of values in old things. New things must stand upon their own merit. They must establish themselves in the minds of people for their worth. Sometimes old and new must be brought into a synthesis for the preservation of an old value in a new idea.

A part of the thrill of living comes through the processes of change. New challenges, opportunities, the expansion of one's intellectual pursuits—all lead to a thrilling experience of life itself. This could have been in the mind of Jesus as he said, "I am not come to destroy, but to fulfill." Fulfillment in this sense means to complete, to continue, to build upon. Modern society must take that which has been handed to it through the accumulative culture and tradition, and build upon it toward a more constructive way of life. Life can be abundant when a full comprehension of the expansion of God's kingdom is realized and when it is realized that his kingdom is an ever-growing, expanding culture for all the ages—every age of mankind.

Change and transition in society happen. This is to say, change is not a planned something, the end result of which is predictable and exact. Change takes place usually without a serious consciousness by those of the social order. Individuals and groups become aware that "things are not as they used to be." Some bemoan this fact. Some become discouraged and cease trying to do much about the old order. Some rationally look the change squarely in the face and adjust a program and life to meet it. Thus, we are always confronted with the necessity of facing frankly what is happening to our society, what is happening to our fellow beings, what is happening to us, and what are the factors that have contributed to these changes.

Anyone whose life spans two, or a part of two, generations in contact with rural America must be aware that many changes have taken place in rural life. These changes have affected home life, community life, church life, and school life. Most of the changes have come gradually, without the masses of the populace being aware of how much the changes have affected the total of life. Consequently, this has resulted in a state of frustration on the part of church, school, and community leaders in many areas. A sense of futility has gripped the mind of many a leader. Others have accepted the challenge of change and are ready to do something about meeting new demands as they arise.

With this brief background, a survey of the changes which have taken place in a nonmetropolitan culture within recent years is presented. A word of definition is necessary before we go further. What is meant by the words "rural" and "urban" and the term "town and country"?

A simple definition of "rural" is all territory outside a Standard Metropolitan Statistical Area where there are fewer than twenty-five hundred people living in a cluster of population known as a town or village. "Urban" is any area in which there are more than twenty-five hundred persons and all area included in a Standard Metropolitan Statistical Area. The SMSA is a city or twin cities of fifty thousand population or more and the surrounding area of one or more counties which are under the trade and work influence of the dominant city. In 1960 there were 212 SMSA's in the nation.

The term "town and country" as used by most denominations usually includes all territory under ten thousand population, and urban includes all territory over ten thousand population. There is a strong tendency, as has been pointed out elsewhere, to think, for administrative purposes, of the work of the church in metropolitan (areas of fifty thousand population or more) or nonmetropolitan areas (areas outside of SMSA's of cities of less than fifty thousand population, including open country).

Rural, however, goes far deeper than simply an arbitrary population dividing line. There is not space here to elaborate the point, but it must be borne in mind that fundamental characteristics of rural life are quite definable in contrast to urbanity.

Rural and urban societies in their complex differences have been a subject of study by sociologists in both Europe and America for almost a century. Literature describing these polar types, rurality and urbanity, is abundant. It is not the purpose of this writing to go into detail on these differences, but since the basic assumption of this work is concerned with the preservation of the church in town and country areas and one of the problems of the church is the blending of rural and urban cultures, a brief review is given as a summary of rural and urban traits.[1]

Rural farm people make their living from agricultural pursuits and are concerned with the producing of raw materials from the soil. Residents in the agricultural town, though not producing from the soil, are so closely related to farm population that weather, seasons, crops, agricultural life are all areas of vital concern. Urban people are interested in the producing of finished products through manufacturing and processing of raw materials. They work by the clock, not by the natural seasons of the year. They are interested in the weather, but only as it affects their physical action, fuel bill, air conditioning, and weekend excursions into the country. Rural people are close to nature and are constantly reminded of the Creator as his world moves through the seasons with unremitting regularity. The urban dweller sees man-made things—buildings, mortar, cement.

The basic unit of rural culture is the family. It works together in making the living and sharing a common enterprise. The neighborhood, composed of a group of families, is a place of sharing mutual needs in times of catastrophe and times of festive enjoyment. Weddings, family dinners, school gatherings, church functions—all bring the families of a neighborhood together. Such associations make for the development of security and personality. The city is not built around the family. Individuality is stressed as the members of the family go their separate ways for work, education, recreation—and often for church.

With the concentration of population in urban areas, there are more incidents of communicable disease, suicide, mental breakdown, and crime than are found in rural areas. The moral state of a predominantly urban culture has been quite sad throughout the history of civilization.

Rural dwellers are traditionally conservative. They revere tradition, custom, and "old things." On the contrary, urban dwellers are concerned with new things, breaking of tradition, exploration. When either trait predominates, a society is in danger. Pure conservatism hampers experimentation, exploration, and progress. Pure liberalism, on the other hand, will lose the "experience of the ages" which has made for depth of living, an appreciation of human values, and a respect for individuality. All that has gone into the development of a traditional culture is not bad. Tried and tested methods of human associations can lead to the discovery of basic ideals to regulate life. To divorce a people from their culture when many traits in that culture have been basically sound in the development of normal, harmonious, and happy living can spell disaster.

Both segments of society, rural and urban, are needed to maintain a healthy balance. Rural areas need the city to develop a technology for modern agricultural methods. No longer is it necessary for the farmer to make his living by "the bending of the back." No longer does the rural dweller have to be deprived in the home of modern conveniences which take away the drudgery of living. Rural life needs the city to absorb its surplus of population, for the rural areas of America are still producing far more children than they can gainfully employ back into their economy. The rural areas need the city to purchase the raw materials for food, fiber, and building.

On the other hand, the city needs the rural area to supply it with the basic materials for manufacturing, for man power, for the food to fill the shelves and refrigerators of its massive supermarkets. Urban areas need the conservative, inherently religious nature of the rural culture to maintain individuality, religiousness, integrity, and morality in the midst of anonymous living. Urban areas need nature—field, stream, lake, mountain, and forest—

as a playground where their dwellers can find release from the tension and drudgery of city living.

With travel by highway, rail, and air, and communications by radio, television, and daily press, there is a constant blending of the above rural-urban traits. A healthy society needs to retain many of the characteristics usually found in rural culture. A nation should strive to preserve "rurality" if for no other reason than to save itself from physical decay.

DEMOGRAPHIC OR POPULATION CHANGES

The 1960 U.S. Census of Population reports brought to light some interesting movements which are taking place in American culture. Some of the movements are not new but have been accelerated during the past decade, while some have been decelerated.

1. There has been a strong movement of population toward the Pacific and the Gulf coasts.

2. There has been a strong movement of population toward the metropolitan areas of the nation.

3. The growth of metropolitan areas has been in the suburban regions outside the central cities.

4. Cities in nonmetropolitan areas, that is, small cities of fifty thousand or less, showed a substantial increase.

5. Many suburban small cities developed, and old towns and cities in suburban areas showed a strong increase in population.

6. In many areas the rural population outside metropolitan areas showed decided loss.

7. Farm population continued to decline.

8. The rural nonfarm population, especially in the

interior sections of the nation, declined. Areas facing the Atlantic, Pacific, and Gulf of Mexico held their own or increased in rural nonfarm population.

9. The Negro population made a dramatic rural-to-urban shift and a South-to-North and West shift. Moreover, it reveals a major suburbanward movement in metropolitan areas.[2]

Much has been written in recent years about the changes which have taken place in the United States in regard to rural-urban, farm-nonfarm population shifts. It is a well-known fact that the farm population of the nation is at an all-time low, compared with the total population of the nation. In 1949 there were 24,194,000 persons, or 16.3 percent of the national population farm. By 1964 there were 12,954,000 persons, or 6.8 percent of the total population farm.[3] There is some discrepancy in comparable figures, however, due to redefinition of farm population. For instance, it is estimated that two fifths of the reported change in rural farm population between 1950 and 1960 was due to a change in method of reporting.

For our purposes, however, as churchmen it must be kept in mind that congregations located in predominantly rural counties will have a much higher percentage farm population than the national average. A case in point is that there are seventy-two counties in Texas which have more than twenty-five percent of the population farm. True, some of the counties are sparsely populated, and most of the counties will have a population no larger than fifteen thousand, but where churches are located in such counties, the membership will be composed of a high percentage of agriculturists. This is to say, the pastor serving a church in the open country or the small town will, in all likelihood, find a large number of the members of the church engaged in agriculture.

A second consideration needs to be made in regard to rural-urban population reporting. On the current basis of population reporting, the urban population between 1950 and 1960 gained 29.3 percent, while the rural population declined 0.8 percent. The 1960 U.S. Census of Population reported 125,269,000 urban population, or nearly seventy percent of the total for the nation, and 54,054,000 rural population. If the same classification of rural-urban had been used in 1960 as was used in 1950, the rural population would have been reported as 69,-964,000, or nearly 16,000,000 more than was reported in the 1960 Census. Most of this 16,000,000 change in reporting came in the growth of suburban districts of formerly small towns which grew into the urban classification. Rural-urban differences are changed at the 2,500 population figure. A decided factor of change is in the reclassification of population by counties that were included in Standard Metropolitan Statistical Areas in 1960 that were not included in 1950. When a county is included in a SMSA, it automatically becomes urban though there may be large segments of rural and rural-farm population in the county. In 1960 there were 212 SMSA's in the nation. This information has been reported, not to defend the rural area, but to clarify the fact that masses of population are still to be served with an adequate church and ministry outside our sprawling American cities. Bogue and Beale report:

However, if one considers the rural population as currently defined in each decade, then rural people remained almost stationary in numbers and lost an amount equivalent to their natural increase from outmovement and the change in the character of communities from rural to urban.[4]

There has been a definite shift in segments of the population in the nonmetropolitan areas of the nation. (Nonmetropolitan is defined as any segment of the population not included in a Standard Metropolitan Statistical Area, which in substance means that there is no city in the region of more than 50,000 population.) Practically all cities of 10,000 to 50,000 increased in population whether in an SMSA or not. In 1960 there were 730 such cities in urban fringe or within SMSA's with a total population of 15,-462,976. There were 810 cities in nonmetropolitan areas with populations 10,000 to 50,000 for a total of 16,172,839.

Most of the cities of 5,000 to 10,000 population in both metropolitan and nonmetropolitan areas increased in population between 1950 and 1960. There were 399 such cities in metropolitan areas with a total of 2,862,099 population, and 995 such cities in nonmetropolitan areas with a total of 6,917,615 population.

Small cities of 2,500 to 5,000 population showed a gain, but not in as large a proportion as cities of larger sizes. In 1960 there were in metropolitan areas 346 cities with populations of 2,500 to 5,000 with a total of 1,250,129 persons. There were 1,806 cities of 2,500 to 5,000 population in nonmetropolitan areas with a total of 6,329,809 persons.

The breaking point, generally speaking, between towns or small cities which held their own, that is, remained relatively constant, lost population, or gained population was around 2,000 population. That is, towns of 2,000 population or less had a good chance to have remained about the same in size, have lost population, or shown a gain. In urbanized areas there were in 1960, 208 towns between 1,000 and 2,000 with a total population of 301,397; and in nonmetropolitan areas there were 3,367 towns between 1,000 and 2,000 population with a total population of 4,748,472.

An often overlooked fact in comparing rural and urban populations is that in 1960 there was a population of 9,851,105 which was classified as urban, but was in open country or towns of less than 1,000 persons. There is a considerable amount of this population engaged in agriculture. It is that part of the urbanized population which has been included in the SMSA's of the nation which, as yet, has not been incorporated into a larger urban center.

Many towns of less than 1,000 population declined between 1950 and 1960. In fact, the smaller the town, the more likely it was that it did decline in population. In nonmetropolitan areas there were in 1960 3,127 towns between 500 and 1,000 population with a total of 2,239,236 persons. There were 4,062 towns between 200 and 500 population with a total of 1,356,570. There were 2,409 towns under 200 population with a total of 297,834 persons. This left 37,465,053 persons in nonmetropolitan areas living in the open country or village of less than 200 population.

When one evaluates the above data, one must be aware of the fact that there is approximately one fifth of all Protestant congregations located in open country or villages under 200 population and practically every town of 200 to 2,500 population (a total of 11,340) will have from one to ten Protestant congregations. The congregations are, on the average, quite small, but nonetheless real. The number of congregations will make up a sizable percentage of the total number of congregations for the major Protestant denominations. Church administration and pastoral administration are operated on the basis of congregational unit rather than number of persons in the congregation. Added to the above data are 2,701 cities in nonmetropolitan areas of 2,500 to 10,000 population. Each of these cities will have from ten to twenty or more Protestant churches. The cities of this size often become the strength of a region economically, politically, socially, and educationally, and can become the centers for religious strength as the congregations become aware of their responsibilities beyond their city limits.

Cities of 10,000 to 25,000 and up to 50,000 outside metropolitan areas are strongholds for the Protestant church. There are 810 cities of this size, and each will have from twenty to forty or more Protestant churches.

As one attempts to define areas of responsibility for the church, there are three major sections which emerge: (1) the central city of more than 50,000 population. This is the incorporated area of a city of more than 50,000 which makes up the core of a Standard Metropolitan Statistical Area. In some cases the central core will be twin cities in which the combined population will be 50,000 or more. (2) The urban fringe area within a SMSA. This is that territory within a SMSA outside the central city but included in the SMSA because of the predominant influence of the central city upon the area economically, politically, and socially. It is in this area that the greatest population expansion in the United States is now taking place. There is also a vast amount of the urban fringe area which is still open country, farmland, and small towns. (3) The nonmetropolitan areas. This can be defined as the area outside one of the nation's 212 SMSA's. Within the nonmetropolitan area there are, for our purposes of church administration, four major population groupings: cities of 10,000 to 50,000; cities of 2,500 to 10,000; towns of 200 to 2,500; and villages and open country with 200 population and less. Table 1 lists the 1960 population data for the above population groupings with some subgroups and the percent of the population in each group.

From Table 1 it can be observed that there are within the United States 23,687 towns of less than 2,500 population outside urbanized areas. There are an additional 3,611 cities of 2,500 to 50,000 population. There are also 37,167,219 persons or 20.8 percent of the nation's population which live in open country outside urbanized areas, and an additional 9,851,105 or 5.5 percent of the population which live in open country or small towns in urbanized areas. (See Figure 3.)

When it is considered that churches are organized according to neighborhood patterns in open country areas and by towns in the nonmetropolitan areas, it is an overwhelming thought to consider the vast number of small churches there are throughout the nation. Population declines and internal changes have affected thousands of congregations in all segments of the population. It must be brought to our attention, however, that population declines do not necessarily reflect a true picture of church membership decline. Time series studies have clearly indicated that the percentage of Protestants in a county becomes larger as the population decreases. This leads one to feel that out-migration is in the nonlandowner and the nonpermanent persons in the rural areas. It also con-

Table 1. U.S. Population by Selected Groups, 1960*

Type of Area	Number of Places	Population	Percent of Total
United States		179,323,175	100.0
Urban total	5,445	125,268,750	69.9
Within Standard Metropolitan Statistical Areas		112,885,178	62.8[3]
Within Urbanized Areas		95,848,487	53.5
Central cities	254	57,975,132	32.4
Urban fringe		37,873,355	21.1
Places 2,500 to 100,000	1,580	27,332,504	15.2
Places less than 2,500	596	689,746	0.4
Other Urban Territory		9,851,105	5.5
Outside Standard Metropolitan Statistical Areas		66,437,997	37.2[3]
Outside Urbanized Areas		83,474,688	46.5
Urban	3,611	29,420,263	16.4
Places of 25,000 or more	200	6,935,191	4.0
Places of 10,000 to 25,000	610	9,237,648	5.2
Places of 5,000 to 10,000[1]	995	6,917,615	3.9
Places of 2,500 to 5,000	1,806	6,329,809	3.3
Rural total[2]		54,054,425	30.1
Places 1,000 to 2,500	4,151	6,496,778	3.3
Places of 2,000 to 2,500	784	1,748,316	1.0
Places of 1,500 to 2,000	1,248	2,157,904	1.2
Places of 1,000 to 1,500	2,119	2,590,568	1.4
Places of 500 to 1,000	3,127	2,239,236	1.3
Places of 200 to 500	4,062	1,356,570	.9
Places under 200	2,409	297,834	.2
Other rural		37,167,219	20.8

* Adapted from U.S. Census of Population 1960. United States Summary, Number of Inhabitants, Tables 5 and 6.

[1] Most major denominations make the distinction between town and country and urban at 10,000 population outside urbanized areas. There is a move, however, to make the distinction metropolitan and non-metropolitan.

[2] The U.S. Census divides rural and urban at 2,500 outside urbanized areas.

[3] According to the latest estimates the population of the U.S. is divided 63.3 percent metropolitan and 36.7 percent nonmetropolitan. SMSA's have increased 7.4 percent, suburban counties outside the central counties in SMSA's increased 11.9 percent, and the total population of the nation

firms the theories proposed by several sociologists that the church in town and country areas is composed of the middle-class, stable, land-owning, business-owning, professional family. These are the people who are established and do not migrate out of areas. Thus, the church in town

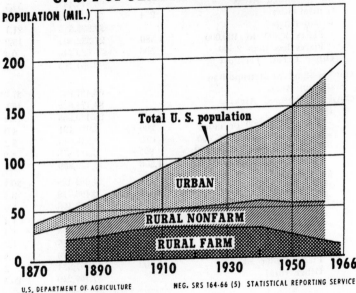

U. S. POPULATION BY RESIDENCE

POPULATION (MIL.)

Total U. S. population

URBAN

RURAL NONFARM

RURAL FARM

1870   1890   1910   1930   1950   1966

U.S. DEPARTMENT OF AGRICULTURE   NEG. SRS 164-66 (5) STATISTICAL REPORTING SERVICE

Figure 3. U.S. Population by Residence. In 1870 the rural farm and rural nonfarm people accounted for a majority of the total population in the United States. A steady shift of proportions of people in rural and urban areas has taken place since. Rural in the above graph refers to persons living in open country or towns of less than 2,500 population outside one of the 212 Standard Metropolitan Statistical Areas.

increased 6.7 percent with an approximate loss of 0.3 percent in non-metropolitan areas. Most of the decrease is in open country and villages of less than 200.

and country areas is not in as poor a state as the out-migration of an area may indicate. It must be said, however, in the light of the above observation, that the structure of church membership is also reflected in the migration patterns. As a general pattern there is a lack of older youth in the church in town and country areas and a predominance of older adults. Exceptions to this, however, are numerous, as new patterns of land settlement, urban fringe developments, new industries moving into small cities and large towns, and recreational centers are taking place.

The internal structure of the various sections of population reveals several interesting trends. The number of young children in a population as compared with the number of women of childbearing age provides an index of the potential growth of a population. The fertility ratio is a means of measuring or providing an index for the child-mother population. The fertility ratio is calculated by dividing the number of children under five years of age by the number of women fifteen to forty-four years of age and multiplying by one thousand. Fertility ratio then is the number of children under five for each one thousand women between fifteen and forty-four years of age. For the white population in the United States in 1960, the fertility ratio was in urban areas 526; rural nonfarm population was 698; and rural farm population was 658. It takes a fertility ratio of approximately 380 for a segment of population to re-populate itself with births over deaths. Hence, each of the major segments of population listed above is large enough not only to re-populate, but to substantially increase the population. It will be noted, however, that the urban population is considerably lower than rural.

57

Figure 4. Age-sex distribution for white and nonwhite population: urban, rural nonfarm, and rural farm, 1960.

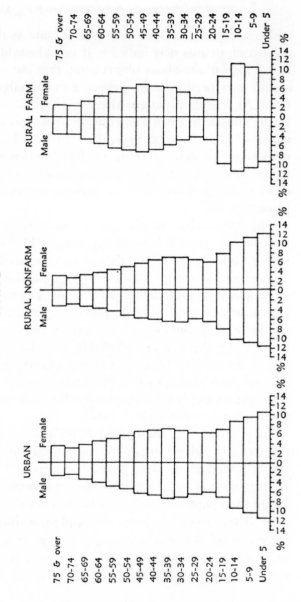

WHITE

NONWHITE

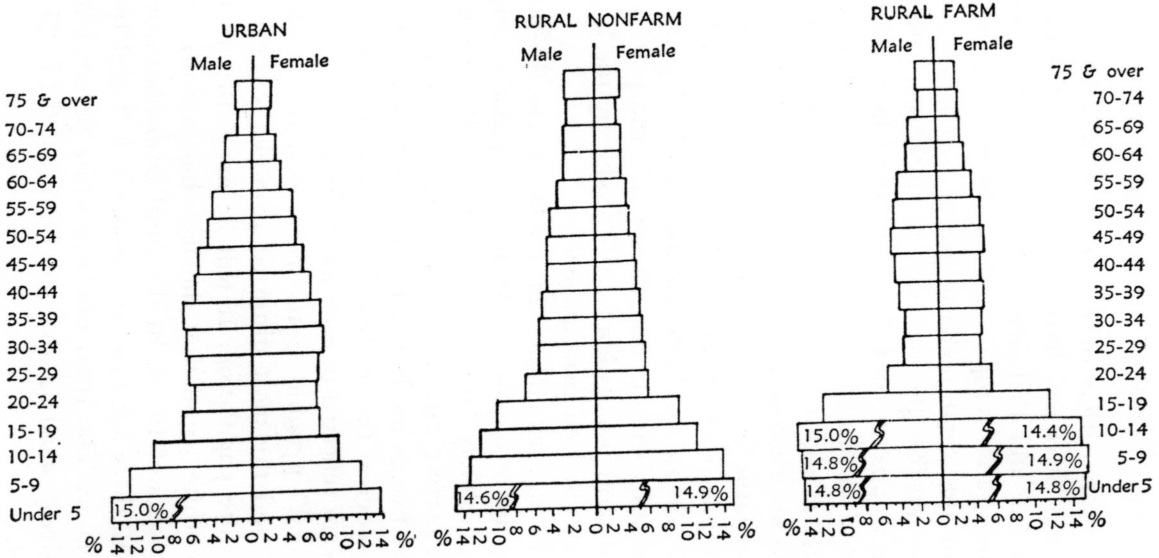

URBAN
Male
Female
RURAL NONFARM
Male
Female
RURAL FARM
Male
Female
75 & over
70-74
65-69
60-64
55-59
50-54
45-49
40-44
35-39
30-34
25-29
20-24
15-19
10-14
5-9
Under 5
15.0%
14.6%
14.9%
15.0%
14.4%
14.8%
14.9%
14.8%
14.8%
% 14 12 10 8 6 4 2 0 2 4 6 8 10 12 14 %

An examination of urban areas will reveal that most central cities will have a much lower fertility ratio than the 526 and that urban fringe areas will have a much higher ratio, comparing favorably with rural ratios.

In the rural nonfarm white population the fertility ratio was 698, the highest in the three segments of population compared, and 658 in the rural farm population.

Within the nonwhite population which in the United States is about ninety-five percent Negroid, the fertility ratio in urban areas was 663; rural nonfarm was 829; and rural farm was 860. These figures reveal that the urban nonwhite resident is beginning to compare favorably with the white in number of children per family. In rural areas large numbers of children are still the pattern, and the rural farm population is still producing the largest number of children percentage-wise.

The age-sex graphs in Figure 4 vividly portray the structure of the three segments of population under study. A completely "normal" age-sex distribution graph will be a perfect pyramid beginning with the base, children under five, as the largest bar and persons seventy-five years and older as the smallest bar with a gradual decline due to death reflected in each bar thereafter. The nearest to a "normal" pyramid is the rural nonfarm white population, and the most distorted pyramid is the rural farm nonwhite population. It will be noted that in the rural farm white population the base bar is shorter than the bars 5–9 and 10–14. In the rural farm nonwhite population all three age brackets—under 5, 5–9, and 10–14—are very large. The rural nonfarm white population is comparatively small in the age brackets 20–24, 25–29, and 30–34.

60

As the 3,134 counties in the United States are examined, it is found that 361 are in Standard Metropolitan Statistical Areas and contain eighty-four percent of the nation's population growth between 1950 and 1960. The trend of population decline that has been taking place since the turn of the century in many predominantly rural counties continued with forty-nine percent of the counties declining between 1950 and 1960, although there was a deceleration of decline in many areas of the nation. The smaller the county population, the more likely it declined; and the larger the county, the more likely it increased. Another corollary is that the more agricultural a county, the more likely it lost population. There are a few exceptions to this corollary, however, especially in areas in which irrigation is supplementing rainfall. The impact of declining rural population continues to be one of the major factors in necessitating new forms of parish administration in the churches located in such regions.

The urban fringe areas showed the most rapid growth in population in the nation between 1950 and 1960. Whereas the central cities had an average growth of 10.7 percent (with several major cities in the nation actually declining, and most of the growth through annexation), the metropolitan ring or urban fringe increased at a rate of 48.6 percent. The urban fringe area is the seat of much transition of older, once rural or town churches to urban. There is much frustration which takes place among the older members of such a church, and there is a heavy demand upon the resources of local boards of church extension to keep abreast of rapid population expansion.

The phenomenal migration of Negro population was

reflected vividly in the 1960 Census. In 1940, for instance, less than half of the Negroes lived in urban areas, and the population was considerably more rural than urban. In 1960, 73.2 percent of the Negro population resided in urban places. Such a radical change in rural areas has thrown an undue burden upon local congregations. Ministerial leadership in the Negro, rural community is depleted and underpaid. There is little incentive for the Negro youth to consider the ministry as a life vocation. Group organizations such as larger parishes, group ministries, and extended ministries need to include Negro congregations in their planning.

TRANSITIONS IN FARM POPULATION

Since the Industrial Revolution which began its major impact about the middle of the last century, the farm population of the nation has undergone radical changes. In a sentence, the changes have been due to mechanization, technology in agricultural methods, and new discoveries for the improvement of seeds and livestock. The percent of farm population in the total national population is at an all-time low, 6.8 percent. At the same time the number of farms has decreased, and the size of farms has increased. (See Figure 5.) Farm output has had a phenomenal increase. Using an index of seventy for farm output in 1940, the output was 112 by 1963. (See Figure 6.) Or to illustrate, corn was produced at an average yield of twenty-nine bushels per acre from 1870 to 1940, rose to 54.5 bushels per acre by 1960, and to 67.3 bushels per acre by 1963. Figure 7 vividly portrays the effects of technological skills when applied to the production of eggs, revealing a seventy percent increase in production between 1940 and 1965.

Such technology has made it possible for one farm worker to supply food and clothing for approximately thirty-one persons by the mid-sixties, whereas only fifteen

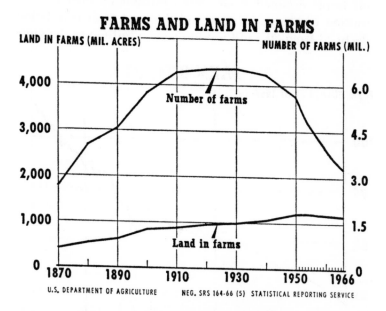

FARMS AND LAND IN FARMS

Figure 5. Farm numbers rose sharply from 1870 to 1910, increasing from less than 3 million to more than 6 million, as agriculture expanded upward. The completion of land settlement in the early 1900's slowed the rate of increase in new farms, and numbers were relatively stable from 1910 to the mid-1930's. A downward trend that became evident about 1940 sharply accelerated after 1950. Numbers were down to slightly more than 3 million by 1966, not much above the 1870 level. The amount of land in farms has steadily increased from 1870 until 1950 with a slight drop between 1950 and 1966.

years before, in 1950, he was supplying needs of 15.4 persons, and in 1940 the number of consumers was 10.7.

The church in the rural section of the population has felt the impact of the technological revolution in a number of ways. In the first place, the number of workers on farms declined from eleven million in 1940 to four million by the mid-sixties, and the total farm population declined from 30.5 million to thirteen million at the same

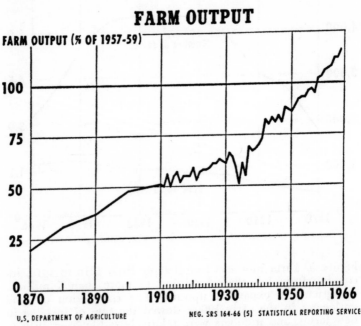

FARM OUTPUT

FARM OUTPUT (% OF 1957-59)

U.S. DEPARTMENT OF AGRICULTURE   NEG. SRS 164-66 (5) STATISTICAL REPORTING SERVICE

Figure 6. Using the index of 100 for the years 1957-1959 for farm output, there has been a steadily upward trend moving from less than 25 in 1870 to nearly 120 by 1965. The drought in the early 1930's produced the only significant period of decline in output during the period. Output after 1940 has followed a rather consistent sharp upward trend.

time. This meant that seventeen million persons were displaced and had to find housing, schools, churches, family employment, and all other necessities of life. Willard Cochrane makes the following observation:

In the short run, then, the migration of this large number of workers and their families away from farming and their resettlement and re-employment in the nonfarm sector has created severe strains. Except in wartime, it has added unemployment and welfare rolls in urban areas. It has contributed to the expansion of city slums, and to all the social adjustment problems associated with slum living. It has wrought havoc in small country towns and forced a reorganization of such rural services as schools, churches, and local government. It has meant business failure and beginning all over again in strange and often degrading circumstances for many families.[5]

For the rural church the above has caused much frustration. However, adjustments are being made, and it behooves churchmen to recognize the need for advance in their churchmanship in the same manner that they have advanced in agricultural technology. Among farm people, with the exception of the extremely conservative, there is an open mind and a willingness to adventure in new things. One of the tragedies in the contemporary scene is the failure of many clergy and denominational executives to be able to challenge the rural laymen with new and meaningful forms of church administration.

Though the number of producing agriculturists is at an all-time low, agriculture remains a basic part of the American economy, providing approximately one fifth of the gross national product of the United States and supplying employment for some thirty percent of the nation's labor force through food and fiber processing and distribution.

SOME OBSERVATIONS

From this brief review of trends in nonmetropolitan America, several observations can be made in regard to the needs of the church.

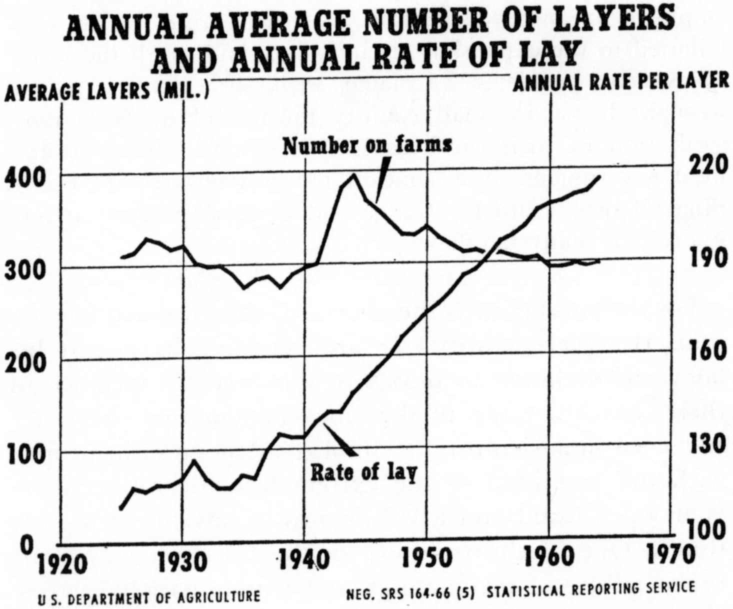

ANNUAL AVERAGE NUMBER OF LAYERS
AND ANNUAL RATE OF LAY

Figure 7. The average annual number of layers on farms moved from a level of about 300 million in the 1920's to a peak of nearly 400 million in 1944. A persistent decline reduced numbers to less than 300 million by the early 1960's. Annual rate of lay has shown a remarkably steady increase since 1940, advancing from about 130 eggs per layer to the record high of nearly 220 by the mid-1960's.

1. Church administration needs to be considered on a larger scale and especially in the centers of population where there are potential leadership and financial resources. Ease of travel and communication makes this possible. Forms of parish structures need to be examined as a means of providing a viable plan for making available a ministry and church for all persons in an area.

2. As churchmen consider their own needs, a careful examination of the trends in the area needs to be made. The root of many problems can be found in the discovery of social and economic trends within an area, and meaningful solutions to the problems can be devised.

3. A vast segment of the American population is outside the major cities, 46.5 percent! Twenty percent, or thirty-seven million persons live in open country or villages of less than two hundred population.

4. With modern technology, a blending of rural and urban influences, the elevation of levels of living, and the increase in educational levels of the nonmetropolitan dweller, the possibilities for new forms of parish structures and a progressive ministry are unlimited.

CHAPTER III

Parish Structures

The word "parish" is defined by Webster in two
manners: (1) a religious congregation comprising all
those who worship together in one church; also, the
district in which they live; (2) in England the ecclesiastical district in charge of a rector or vicar. In these two
definitions we have summed up the concept of parish
as it is normally thought of in the United States. The
word "parish" conveys the idea of a local congregation
but also a territory around a local church for which that
congregation has responsibility. In England the parish idea
conveys with it the concept that the parish priest or vicar
is responsible for ministering to all the persons who live
within a certain geographic region. This concept is con-
veyed through the Roman Catholic Church and is strictly
adhered to in that when a Catholic family moves from

one parish to another, its membership is automatically changed. The Protestant church with its spirit of freedom has never adhered strictly to this concept in America. Parish lines may be drawn for administrative purposes, but by and large, all persons who are members of the church have the right to belong to any church of their choice. Without a state church or a strong ecclesiastical overarching body to enforce parish structure, the freedom of choice concept will remain in American life. Some denominations have made attempts at defining a parish, such as The Methodist Church in the 1964 *Discipline* in Par. 104.3: "A **parish** shall be identified as an area of service with the membership constituency of one or more local churches having a co-ordinated program and organization to fulfill a ministry directed to all the people of the area. It may include local churches of other denominations." Most concepts of parish as defined above are caught in this definition. It is to the concept of parish that we wish to speak in this chapter.

By parish we are thinking of that territory for which a denominational or interdenominational program of church work should have program and administrative responsibility. This may consist of a rather small area or a comparatively large area depending upon density of population, the potential for evangelization, and the natural sociological groupings as described in Chapter I. Too many congregations and pastors conceive of the work of their church as being limited to its present constituency. In other words, many people are left out of the parish because they have not made an overt attempt to become a part of an organized membership. If we can bear in mind this concept of parish, then we can look forward to various types of organization to perform a ministry of greater service to all persons who are within the geographic area under consideration for ministry. Several types of organizations will be presented with some detail in order to present a clearer definition of the parish ministry.

THE CONSOLIDATED CHURCH

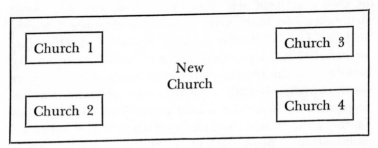

The consolidated church consists of two or more congregations of the same or of different denominations which work out an agreement of consolidation whereby a new congregation is brought into being. In some cases a new building is erected, or in other cases two or more buildings are put together to form a more substantial building. In some cases a church will consolidate with another existing church and be absorbed into the membership of that existing church. In this case the building of the church into which the congregation is moving will become the home for the new congregation.

Through recent years there has been a tendency on the part of many persons in small open country churches to rebel against the concept of consolidation. It has in many cases been a rebellion against the encroachment of authority from the outside and a feeling of animosity, particularly toward those persons located in towns. In more recent years, however, the animosities of rural and urban people have been diminished until in many cases there is much cooperation taking place prior to a time of consolidation of the churches. There is much precedent for consolidation that has taken place in our public school systems in America. There has been much rebellion against consolidation of schools in many sections of the country; but as consolidation has taken place, many persons have felt that the advantages of a larger school with a stronger teaching staff and more adequate building have been worth the price that has been paid for the giving up of individual, one-room schools. Sometimes, however, persons have felt that the autonomy of the individual was destroyed and that something went out of the neighborhood when the school left. In recent years I have discovered many places where church consolidation has taken place with very little fanfare or pressure by denominational executives. Local congregations have come to realize that a neighborhood has disintegrated and the time for the open country church to move its constituency bodily into another congregation has come about. Frequently, this has been a very happy situation and usually results in the preservation of most of the people in the churches under consolidation. A case in point is an east Texas congregation in a town of about three hundred population which is now composed of the town church plus four open country churches that have consolidated into the town church. The leadership prior to consolidation was so integrated into the life of the area that they were accepted into the leadership of the town church

71

without any difficulty. Many times there are family ties and kin relationships which make such consolidation quite easy.

Consolidation should never be forced upon a neighborhood church. This cannot be said too strongly, for to force consolidation from the outside or by denominational executives is to cause great confusion and many times undue anxiety and antagonism. Studies have revealed that when a consolidation is forced, ordinarily only ten to twenty percent of the people will cooperate in the consolidation. This leaves a large number of people unchurched, or else they have to seek another church. Similar studies have revealed that when consolidation comes from the inner desires of the congregations involved, most likely eighty to ninety percent of the people will go along with the consolidation.

It has been estimated by persons in the field of research that approximately two thousand churches per year have been closing in rural areas across America for the past twenty to twenty-five years. This, no doubt, is a true estimate and more than an educated guess. The question remains: What happens to the people when a church closes? Are they left without a church, are they happily integrated into the life of another congregation, or are they consolidated into the life of one or more congregations? Throughout this work we have attempted to carry the concept that the parish is responsibility territory for some congregation. When a church ceases to be, there ought always to be some form or organization which is standing ready to minister to the persons in that geographic region. If consolidation is the answer, then there needs to be some kind of an alert method by which people

72

will be brought into an understanding of one another. Some of the forms of cooperation described below are means of bringing persons into a vital relationship so that they understand one another sufficiently well to move together eventually toward consolidation. It is the belief of this author that if a rural church is needed to maintain a neighborhood solidarity and a spirit of community among a people, even though the congregation may become quite small, there should be every effort to continue a partial ministry in the local church. It is possible that a partial ministry can be maintained in a local church and a fuller ministry in one of the cooperative ministries described below.

The Extended Ministry

Small city or a town church	One pastor	Rural church

The extended ministry (sometimes called the extension church, the outpost, or other terms) consists of a strong town church sharing its ministry with another church. In recent years in some sections of the nation the extended ministry has been the means of ministering to thousands of people who otherwise would have been isolated from a strong ministry. Frequently, a small country church finds itself orphaned because other churches on the pastoral charge have either ceased to be or have become strong enough to employ a pastor on a full-time basis. The small church is not strong enough to support a full-time pastor, and even if it did have the financial resources, there would not be enough work for a minister to perform in being the pastor of such a small congregation.

The extended ministry is a process by which a town church accepts the responsibility for ministering unto another church which is close enough for the pastor or staff to perform Sunday activities as well as weekday ministries. As has been described in the chapter dealing with the nature of nonmetropolitan areas, many small churches have been established which now are five to ten miles from town. Good highways have been built which make it possible for a minister to be in a country church at an early hour and back in the town church within five to ten minutes' time for another service of worship. Again the concept of parish is brought into mind as the town church assumes the responsibility for serving persons within the geographic area by extending its ministry farther out into the countryside. The normal structure for such organization consists of: (1) one pastor, or pastor and employed staff; (2) two or more congregations under the direction of one pastor or staff; (3) a strong town or small city church sharing its ministerial leadership with one or more churches. The second church may have a complete organization or a partial organization depending upon size and leadership potential, and it should pay a proportionate share of the pastor's salary and denominational items.

Denominational bodies need to establish policies in regard to extended ministries and any other form of parish organization. This means that the denominational body needs to draw up specific statements concerning pastors who serve in extended ministries in regard to salary base and other remuneration. This is particularly true in episcopal forms of government where salary base becomes a major item in regard to appointments. The salary which is paid by the second church needs to be considered as a part of the basic total salary of the pastor; and when a pastor is brought into the new situation, it should be explained to him that the second church is a part of the pastoral appointment. Tragedy has resulted when this is not the case, and the pastor feels that he has had something added to his load after being appointed.

Sometimes one of the major problems that is faced in the extended ministry is the attitude of the congregation in the town church. Frequently, church leaders will say, "We have employed our pastor for our church, not for a second church." There is also in some areas of the country a stigma in that for a minister to serve more than one congregation is a lesser appointment. Fortunately, in many cases, these attitudes have been overcome, and the town church recognizes a parish responsibility and is willing to share its pastor with the people in the second church. In all likelihood the only part of the program of the church that the pastor may miss is some of the church school in the town church. Church schools traditionally have been lay organizations and should be able to stand on their own administrative leadership without having to demand the time of the pastor to be present. Thousands of rural churches for fifty years have maintained their Sunday schools without the assistance of a pastor, and in many cases the town church now can assume the leadership of the church school without the pastor's presence on Sunday morning. There is much to be gained by the consideration of the extended ministry by town and small city churches across America as they extend their parish boundaries to include areas where there are small open country churches and other churches nearby which need a ministry.

THE ENLARGED CHARGE
(Sometimes called the Larger
Charge or Cooperative Charge)

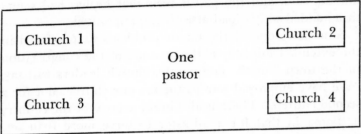

The enlarged charge consists of two or more congregations under the direction of one pastor operating as one unit with several places for services of worship. Again, the concept of the parish is brought into play as one thinks of an enlarged charge. The enlarged charge is a situation in which there are several congregations of one denomination or of several denominations which decide to cooperate in a program whereby they employ one pastor to serve all the churches. Rather than each church functioning as a separate unit, however, they maintain their separate units in their local buildings and localities, but actually perform the services of the church on a parish-wide basis. Autonomy is maintained in each local congregation, but cooperation is forthcoming in the total life and program of the total parish involving all congregations. The great advantages of such an arrangement lie in the fact that a fuller program of church activities can be promoted than can be done for individual congregations. The structure of an enlarged charge is given below:

1. There is an organization within each congregation consisting of official boards, various committees or commissions, women's work, men's work, youth work. The members of various organizations in the local congregation shall automatically be members of a charge-wide organization. In other words, the charge is organized as one church would be with separate executive bodies in each local congregation. For more effective work the local congregation may form a coordinated parish-wide organization and provide representatives for the parish-wide official board and other suborganizations within the parish. Coordinated planning shall be done on a parish-wide basis.

2. Each congregation shall have a budget consisting of local expenses, such as building maintenance, utilities, custodial service, insurance, and a sum to contribute to the parish-wide budget which shall include ministerial support, missionary offerings, and other denominational expenses. A sum should be included in the latter for pastor's office and travel expense, a parish paper, parsonage maintenance, and other parish-wide interests.

3. There shall be a central parish treasurer who shall receive from each local church the appropriate amount for the parish budget. The central treasurer shall disperse funds of the parish treasury consisting of ministerial support, missions, and other connectional items as well as parsonage expense, pastor's travel, office expense, and so forth. It can be seen that the statement of the budget described in item 2, which includes the ministerial support and denominational expenses as well as any item which concerns the entire parish, is sent to a central

treasurer. The amount that each congregation shares in the total expenses of the parish is prorated on the ability of the congregation to pay rather than on the amount that the congregation receives of the pastor's time and ministry. Worship service schedules and other ministries of the pastor are worked out through the coordinating council.

4. As much as possible shall be done on a parish-wide basis in overall planning and work. For instance, the women's organization can be established on a parish-wide basis with circles in each local church. Training schools, youth activities, men's groups, evangelistic programs, and all other phases of the church can be planned on a parish-wide basis. There should be a parish paper distributed to all homes in all churches at least once a month.

One of the main advantages of an enlarged charge is the feeling that individuals receive by being a part of a dynamic whole. There is also the aspect of all the congregations serving all of the people within the parish area. No longer is each congregation a separate unit; instead, each is a part of a total body attempting to serve all of the people and their needs.

THE LARGER PARISH

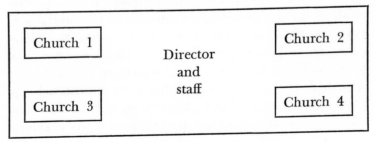

Probably the easiest way to define a larger parish is to refer back to the description of the enlarged charge and conceive of the charge being served by a staff of employed persons rather than one minister. Therefore, we would say that the larger parish is defined as an enlarged charge with the additional characteristics:

1. A multiple staff of ministerial and professional leadership serving all the congregations. The leadership may consist of assistant pastors, director of education, director of evangelism, and so forth.

2. There may be, though not necessarily, congregations of different denominations.

3. There will usually be a constitution controlling the work of the parish.

The larger parish had its origin in 1910 in Benzonia, Michigan, with a minister by the name of Harlow S. Mills. Mills had suffered the loss of his wife by death and was under a particular strain of adjustment when he received an invitation from the Congregational denomination to become an executive in the central office of the church. Pondering whether he should accept the position or whether he should stay with his Benzonia church, he conceived of the idea of the Benzonia church reaching out to serve a larger area. Through his concepts of the larger parish, a very fruitful ministry came into being with assistance in various fields of ministerial service. Mills had five convictions concerning the work of the church in town and country areas: (1) The real object of the church is to serve people, and its claim for support should rest upon the same ground upon which every other institution bases its claim for support—that it gives value received; (2) the church must serve all people within a given

79

geographic area; (3) the church must serve all the interests of the people; (4) the village, if it would fulfill its mission, must be responsible for the country evangelization; and (5) if the village church would fulfill its mission, it must be a community church.[1]

The above five visions may sound quite obvious to the present-day church administrator, but in Mills's day they were revolutionary. The philosophy undergirding the larger parish was that the central or town church should share its pastor, finances, and resources of leadership with the entire countryside in order that the total population could be effected for the cause of the Christian faith. No individual was to be left out of the responsibility of the church. No individual needs were to be ignored. This meant that if the needs were physical, they became the church's responsibility. If the need was for a better agriculture, this was the task of the church. Mills felt that the church must be a service institution. It deserved to be supported in proportion to the services provided to its members and community.

By 1925 there was a sufficient number of larger parishes for Edmund deS. Brunner, who was employed by the Institute of Social and Religious Research, to make a study of larger parishes. His findings were published in a book entitled *The Larger Parish, a Movement or an Enthusiasm?* [2] Brunner found only eighty-four larger parishes, though several hundred were reported to be in existence. The skeptical title of his book reveals the uncertainty about the movement. The study was valuable in that it did make a contribution to the basic assumptions that should go into the establishing of larger parishes. Brunner stated that there were nine areas of concern in establishing and maintaining larger parishes. These are:

1. The territory included is an economic and/or social unit.

2. The territory has adequate resources, under normal economic conditions, in order to support the larger parish sooner or later.

3. The churches of the parish combine their finances, at least those regarding the salary of the staff and preferably for all items.

4. The staff consists of two or more persons with special training or interest in the field of responsibility to which each is assigned.

5. There is a functioning parish council.

6. The parish gives, or at least sincerely aims to give, many-sided service to the whole territory it serves and to every person within it.

7. The parish has exclusive possession of its field so far as Protestant work is concerned, or at least has cooperative relations with other religious groups and with community organizations.

8. The parish recognizes its interdenominational obligations.

9. The parish is assured of the continued support of the denomination or denominations concerned regardless of changes in administrative personnel.[3]

In 1939 the New York State College of Agriculture produced a bulletin entitled *The Larger Parish, an Effective Organization for Rural Churches.*[4] The bulletin was a condensation of the findings from a doctoral dissertation by Mark Rich. Three larger parishes were the basis of the study, but the entire scope of the larger parish movement was surveyed. The bulletin had widespread circulation and did much to foster the larger parish movement. Rich states, "A larger parish is a group of churches in a large community or a potential religious community, working together through a larger parish council and a larger parish staff to serve the people of the area with a diversified ministry." [5] An examination of this statement reveals three fundamental ideas in the concept of a larger parish. (1) the community; (2) bona fide interchurch cooperation; and (3) a specialization in training and service among the professional leaders.

In more recent times the larger parish has come to be accepted by many denominations as a means of serving a large constituency of people within a given geographic area with a multiple staff of trained leaders to bring a total and effective program of the work of the church to its constituents. A bibliography at the end of this work will contain other publications in the field of the larger parish.

THE GROUP MINISTRY

Charge 1	Charge 2	Charge 3
Pastor	Pastor	Pastor
Director	Church A	Church A
Church A	Church B	Church B
Church B	Church C	Church C

The group ministry consists of two or more independent pastoral charges working cooperatively for the development of the work of the church in a given area. The group ministry is different from the larger parish in that each of the ministers in the group ministry is responsible for a pastoral charge of his own. Work is done on a cooperative basis rather than on a closely integrated, organized basis for all churches involved. The characteristics of a group ministry may be summarized as follows:

1. Two or more charges working cooperatively. It is best if the churches are located in one enlarged, rural community (locality group III—one dominant town and one or more subdominant towns).

2. A lay and ministerial council to guide the work of the organization is elected with representatives from each church.

3. Each minister serves a pastoral charge and derives his support from the charge.

4. There is a central budget for any unified program such as a newspaper, rural worker, or other items of common concern.

5. A director is elected by the lay council or appointed by the appropriate denominational executive.

The group ministry had its origin in October of 1938 with the publication of a bulletin entitled "The Group Ministry," written by Aaron H. Rapking. Rapking had joined the staff of the Division of National Missions of the Board of Missions of The Methodist Church in 1938. He started to make a visual record of existing larger parishes in the United States and discovered that there was such diversity in the types of programs in operation that it was going to be virtually impossible to get any kind of documentation which would be meaningful. He called together a group of persons interested in the field of town and country church for consultation, and out of the consultation came the idea of the group ministry. Rapking summarizes his findings in the following quotation which is taken from his unpublished autobiography:

In many town and country areas that have the same major trading, recreational, educational, and cultural centers there are from three to six Methodist ministers and from twelve to twenty-four churches.

Here is a word picture of my basic conception of the group ministry that I presented to the group: The appointment of our ministers to a regular charge in a recognized natural area such as a county seat town or trade center surrounded by communities and neighborhoods with the understanding that while they would do the work of a good minister of Jesus Christ on their charge, they would also work with other character building organizations to study and promote certain activities in the interest of coming to grips with the problems, the needs, and opportunities of the people and thus help bring the kingdom of God's ideals and attitudes into action in the total life of the area. One minister in the group might be strong in evangelism; another in dealing with people; while another's specialty might be that of promoting the redemptive process through Christian education. These ministers would meet every two weeks and with a map of the territory before them, study, pray, and plan to promote those projects and grapple with those problems, the solution of which would mean much to the building of the kingdom of God in the area and in the world.

As there is need for ministers to work together in a community or natural area, so there is great need for laymen and churches to join hands and work together to combat evil, promote, strengthen, and make more effective the program of the churches in the area. The establishing of a Methodist Fellowship Council did not call for a change in the present local or district church setup. The council would be established by electing one man, one woman, and one young person under twenty-four years of age from each church cooperating. The council should meet at least four times a year. The ministers would be members of the council. Committees on survey, evangelism, Christian education, music, plays and pageants, stewardship, recreation, cooperation with other agencies could be appointed as needed.[6]

Though the term "larger parish" originated in the Congregational ministry and the term "group ministry" originated in The Methodist Church, both terms have become broader in their concept and scope and have been applied to any kind of work done in the general structure or pattern and with one or more denominations cooperating. It is interesting also to note that both terms have now been adopted by a number of denominations for work within the inner city parishes. The latter is a revelation of the fact that the larger parish and group ministry are concepts of parish administration which are applicable in any area of ministry in metropolitan or nonmetropolitan areas. Within many cities the concept of group ministry has taken hold, not only in inner city but in all sections of the city.[7] Within a given geographic region which has some homogeneous continuity, six or eight churches are banding themselves together to do cooperatively what they cannot do individually. In many cases programs such as nursery schools, health clinics, the relief of those who are in physical need, and joint programs of evangelism are undertaken.

The Yoked Field

Church 1 of denomination 1	One pastor	Church 2 of denomination 2

The yoked field consists of two congregations of different denominations served by one pastor. Each church maintains separate budgets for denominational and missionary work, but cooperates on pastor's salary and mutual work.

The yoked field has proved to be quite valuable in areas in which the denominational programs have disintegrated to the point that there are not enough churches of one denomination to maintain a strong pastoral unit. By yoking together it is possible to call a minister to serve both churches with an adequate salary and housing. Individual autonomy is retained by each congregation by its maintenance of its own denominational connections and support of its denominational programs.

The one problem that arises with the yoked field is determining what denomination will supply the ministry. It sounds good to say that one denomination will supply the ministry for four years and then the other denomination for another four years. Congregations need to remember that ministers may find themselves in a predicament with their own denomination if they have stepped out of line of an ordinary pastoral situation. This is particularly true with persons in the episcopal form of government. Therefore, it is wise for the two churches to determine in advance which denomination they will ask to supply the minister. This denomination then becomes responsible for supplying the minister as long as the yoked field is in operation. It is possible that after a few years both churches will become a part of the one denomina-nation which in reality is quite good if it can be done without too much friction. This, of course, is not the ulti-mate aim, but this sort of arrangement does sometime eventuate.

THE FEDERATED CHURCH

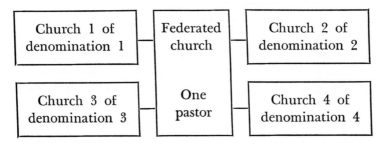

The federated church consists of two or more congrega-tions of different denominations which unite to form one congregation under Articles of Federation. Within the United States in the last thirty years there have been many churches which have federated. This has been done in cities where different denominational churches have united in one neighborhood in order to make a more effective ministry. It has been done in many small towns where there are three or four denominations competing with one another in a community that is strong enough to support one church, but not three or four. The federated church has had its successes and failures, like any other program of cooperative action. Some denominational leaders feel that it is not an effective way of solving the problems of the churches in town and country areas, while others feel that it is an effective type of organization and makes for good ecumenical action. With the rising impetus upon interchurch cooperation and the ecumenical movement, the federated church has the potential of strengthening the work of the church in many communities.

The federated church operates under Articles of Federation which in reality make up a constitution. The Articles of Federation define (1) the method by which a pastor is selected; (2) the conditions of church membership and dismissal from the congregation; (3) the adoption of rituals of receiving members into the church, baptism, the sacrament of the Lord's Supper, the solemnization of matrimony, and the burial of the dead (ordinarily such rituals are taken either from the denomination of one of the cooperating churches or one of the various ecumenical rituals that have now been produced); (4) directives regarding church school literature; (5) directives in regard to the appropriation of missionary funds; (6) denominational cooperation of the various denominations involved.

It can be readily seen that with so many areas in which some kind of consensus of opinion must be established by all of the cooperating bodies that there are many opportunities for friction and discord in the federated church. The buildings alone sometimes prove to be a stumbling block. Which congregation will give up its building to be meeting in another building? What will be done with the buildings that are abandoned? Some of the most effective federated churches have met the problem by moving the buildings bodily to the site of one or to an entirely new site and uniting them in the major plant for the operation of the church. In some cases all buildings have been abandoned, and a new building has been erected.

One of the major problems that is faced in the federated church, like that of the yoked field, is the problem of which denomination will provide a ministry. Again, it looks good in the Articles of Federation to provide that each denomination shall supply a pastor for a stated period of time in a rotating system. But again, the pastors who are willing to accept such a temporary arrangement may find it difficult at the end of their term of office to be brought back into line in their own denomination. It is far better if the Articles of Federation will state that one of the cooperating denominations is to supply the pastor from the beginning and for all time.

Many years ago in the state of Iowa the Iowa Council of Churches established in their Comity Committee "a rule of thumb" that they would assist any local community in establishing a federated church provided the local community would ask the Comity Committee to make a study of the community and determine which denomination should then be responsible for supplying a ministry. This actually takes the responsibility out of the hands of the local people. This has worked quite effectively in several situations in the state.

The federated church has not served its day and should be considered as one of the means of cooperation in communities that are strong enough to support one church but not several.

THE RELATIONSHIP OF LOCALITY GROUPS
AND TYPES OF CHURCH ORGANIZATION

The consolidated church, the extended ministry, the enlarged charge, the larger parish, the yoked field, and the federated church ought to be confined to one community as described under locality group II in the first chapter of this work. Locality group II, as will be recalled, is the rural community. It consists of one town and its surrounding area in which there are a number of rural neighborhoods (locality group I). Ordinarily the human ties of people in such a closely associated group of relationships are sufficient enough to make for close cooperation. It will be recalled that one of the basic problems that Edmund deS. Brunner discovered in his study in 1933 was the fact that many larger parishes had tried to extend themselves too far and had gone beyond the community boundaries. Where there are natural associations such as common trade centers, schools, recreational centers, hospital centers, and other forms of human interaction, it is not too difficult to get some kind of cooperation among the people involved. Leaders need to take this into account and make a very careful analysis of the community patterns before attempting to make any kind of close cooperation.

The group ministry can operate on the basis of an enlarged community or locality group III. Since each pastoral charge is a unit unto itself and in all likelihood will be involved in its own locality group II, the associations of people on the larger basis are not as strong. However, they do not need to be as strong in the group ministry as in the larger parish. Frequently, locality group

III will be coterminus with a county or portion of a county in which there is one larger town or small city and several smaller towns, all of which are dependent upon one another for mutual trade and existence.

It should be kept in mind always that any form of church cooperation is basically a philosophy of service to the people within a given geographic area. It is secondly an organization. The idea of *parish* needs to be emphasized again when one is thinking of a group of persons in a given geographic area who are bound together with a common force and decide to work together for the good of the total cause. Three words stand out in relationship to any kind of work within the parish structure. First, *consolidation* of every phase of the activities of the local church which is feasible. This strengthens the congregations in every phase of church activity. Second, *coordination* of the work of the churches within the area. Where consolidation cannot take place, coordination is feasible, bringing about the work of all congregations in a coordinated fashion to strengthen the life of the individual Christian in his expression of faith. Third, *cooperation* in every phase of activity where consolidation and coordination cannot be effected. Cooperation means working together in a manner which expresses the fundamental belief of the areas we have in common cause with one another as Christian believers.

Establishing
the Cooperative Parish

Through personal conversation and correspondence with forty denominational executives in church and community or town and country work, I found that the universal request was for a more detailed analysis of the process by which a cooperative parish is brought into being. How can the change be brought about whereby a congregation or two or more congregations will create and accept a more effective form of ministry?

A Construct of Social Action

The truth is that change is taking place. Change is inevitable in every segment of society. The questions are in what direction will the change take place, how rapidly will it take place, and how can change be directed so that it will be for the advantage of the individual and society, including the church? Change, to a certain degree, can be controlled, or at least can be used to an advantage for the good of individuals. Leaders in the church need to understand the basic principles involved in change and social control. Individuals will ordinarily act when they feel their action is for personal and family advantage. The same is true in corporate or group situations. In other words, persons will act in a group if they feel such action is for the betterment of the group. This is true with a congregation in a local church. The question then before us is how are congregations made aware of social change which has affected the church, and how can congregations recognize the need for creative thinking and adoption of new forms of ministry to meet new needs?

Social scientists have devised various patterns by which social change can be effected. No plan is all-inclusive or a panacea for all of the problems involved. One always has to take into account the human will and tradition. Frequently, the traditions associated with the church are the deepest and most difficult to overcome. However, church leaders can profit greatly by understanding the process of social change and can use some of the findings of social scientists to an advantage in establishing cooperative parishes.

One of the most concise and descriptive analyses of the process of social change is that devised by George M. Beal and his associates at Iowa State University of Science and Technology. The diagram, Figure 8, gives a framework for social action. It is suggested that one read through the diagram from left to right and then return

93

to the following description for an understanding of the chart.

The numbers 1, 2, 3, 4, etc., represent the steps in social action with each step being a foundation for the next step. There are, in addition to the stages in social action, some important considerations which run throughout the various stages. These are listed A, B, C, etc.

Now to consider the stages: 1. The social systems. All social action takes place within the context of existing social systems. For our consideration we think of the church itself as a social system, and we also think of the area in which the church is located. The areas are described in Chapter I as locality groups I, II, III, IV. In addition to the church and the locality groups there are subsystems such as power structures, formal and informal groups, social stratifications, governments, and interrelated areas of each.

2. Convergence of interests. All social action begins when the interest and definition of need on the part of two or more people converge and are brought together. Usually convergence of interest begins with a small group of people. In the case of the church this can be two or more laymen, two or more ministers, a minister and one or more laymen, denominational executives, a regional church body such as a board of missions or town and country commission. In other words, the convergence of interest may be stimulated by people within the system (church or churches) or persons from without the system (district superintendent, regional missionary, executive secretary for a regional church board, and so forth). Once there has been a convergence of opinion, there needs to be some tentative definition of goals which are suffi-

ciently defined and agreed upon for continued social action and exploration.

3. Analysis of the prior social system. In most situations there will be existing churches, remnants of past churches or past traditions that need to be examined. Traditional patterns of successful and unsuccessful communication and cooperation will have been established. At this stage the persons seeking change (change agents) need to ask the following questions: (a) Has there in the past been a similar kind of project proposed? Was it successful? If so, what factor contributed to its success? If it was not successful, why not? The intent of these questions is to capitalize on former successes and to avoid former mistakes. (b) What types of cooperative projects have the people in the area undertaken before? What was their success, and how were they brought about? Such projects could be school consolidation, organization of a cooperative or a community council, and similar movements. (c) What is the general attitude of the people in the area toward progress? Is there is a defeatist attitude, or are people optimistic about change? (d) What churches seem to work best together? Is there ill feeling between some churches which may prevent them from working together on a cooperative basis?

4. Delineation of relevant social systems (local churches and church bodies). Very few cooperative parishes will include all of the churches of all of the denominations within the area. It is well to study the churches of the area to see how many and which ones are needed in the cooperative parish to meet the needs or goals looked for. Some congregations will automatically eliminate themselves due to denominational policies. Other congregations

will not feel the need for a cooperative parish, but the group promoting the investigation may feel they are needed. Both those churches which are interested in and those opposed to a cooperative parish need to be taken into consideration and be invited to participate in the process. Denominational executives such as bishops, district superintendents, area directors, executive secretaries of area boards and agencies need to be brought into the early stages of planning. Their attitude toward the project must be known and taken into account.

5. The initiating set. Up to this stage only a few persons have been involved, and they have operated primarily through conversation and without authority. An "initiating set" needs, now, to be selected. In initiating a cooperative parish, the initiating set can be selected by electing or appointing a small delegation, one to three persons, from each congregation. Other strategic persons such as pastors and denominational representatives will need to be on the initiating set or planning committee.

6. Legitimation. Legitimation is used here mainly in the sense of giving sanction for action. The sanction may be formal authority or an understanding for action. Within the initiating set described in 5, there will be persons who are influential in a community action program such as the development of a cooperative parish. Such persons may or may not be influential people for other community action projects, but it is well to know where persons stand in regard to their influence with persons in their respective congregations. Every church and community have influential persons who, in a sense, are the decision-makers for their group. Such persons can be instrumental in the success or failure of a cooperative parish because of the

96

A CONSTRUCT OF SOCIAL ACTION - PART I

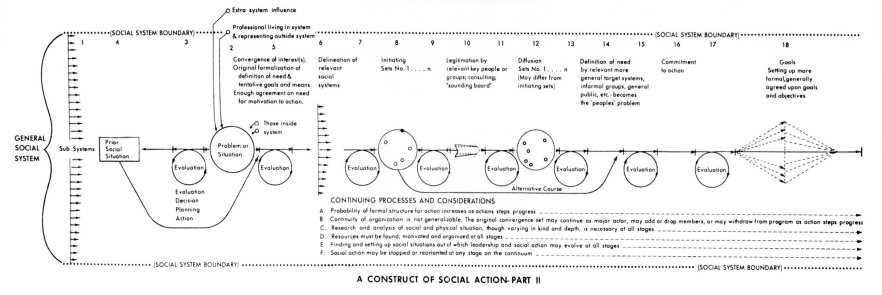

A CONSTRUCT OF SOCIAL ACTION - PART II

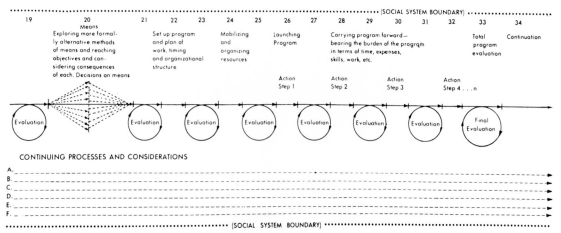

Figure 8. A Construct of Social Action.

From George M. Beal, "Social Action: Instigated Social Change in Large Social Systems," in James H. Copp, ed., *Our Changing Rural Society* (Ames, Iowa: Iowa State University Press, 1964). Both this chart and the material describing the process of social action are adapted from Mr. Beal's article.

personal influence they have with the members of the congregation.

7. The diffusion set. At step 7 in the social action process more people are brought into the planning. The initiating set, or committee from each church, will now need to convey the information back to the local congregation of what has taken place thus far. It is a good time to inform local church official boards and as many members of the congregation as possible of the planning to this stage. It is also a good time for evaluation to take place of what has been done so far and exploration of what further steps need to be taken. A sound principle for social action has been suggested as 5 P's: Prior Planning Prevents Poor Performance.

8. Definition of need by more general relevant groups and organizations. Step 8 is that of broadening the base of knowledge of persons who are to be involved in the cooperative parish. It calls for: (a) basic education of all persons to be involved in the parish. This is done through "house groups" where small groups of laymen are invited to participate in discussions, newsletters, public press, discussion in church school, and other church gatherings; (b) a questionnaire to all families involved, asking for basic information concerning the family, community activity participation, the work of each church and its effectiveness in the community, and so forth; (c) a look at other similar cooperative parishes as a means of stimulating action. Lay speakers from similar cooperative parishes where a measure of success has been forthcoming may be helpful.

9. Decisions (commitments) to action by each congregation. Each congregation is given the opportunity to

vote if it will become a participating group in the cooperative parish. If thorough planning has taken place, congregations will be ready to make the decision for cooperation. At this stage there is still enough flexibility that much work is yet to be done, and congregations need to understand that they will have a part in setting up the final form or organization. They, at this stage, are committed to an idea with somewhat of an "on trial" participation.

10. Formulation of objectives.

11. Decision on means to be used.

12. Plan of work.

13. Mobilizing resources. Representatives from each participating congregation need to formulate the definite objectives of the group organization and to establish a framework by which the objectives can be attained. This will, in all likelihood, result in a constitution and bylaws to give direction to the parish. (See a sample constitution in Appendix A.) The constitution will give a general framework of organization, responsibilities, financial support, communications, committee structure, and so forth.

14. Action. The final stage is action. The cooperative parish comes into being and begins functioning as a parish.

15. Evaluation. At every stage careful evaluation needs to be made by examining progress and next steps. After a parish has functioned for a few months, the evaluation process needs to be brought into focus. Mistakes will be made, and the earlier they are caught, the better. It will be discovered that there are areas of need which have not been provided for. The parish council and the parish staff need to be in a constant state of evaluation to be sensitive to emerging needs.

In the chart will be seen a series of ABC's under the heading Continuing Processes and Considerations. These involve preparation of organizational structures, continuity of the organization, research and analysis, mobilizing resources, discovering leadership in each church, and the changing of social action at any stage in the process. The above areas need to be considered throughout the entire process. Chapter VII is devoted to the necessary research in planning the cooperative parish.

Needless to say, the above process is long and detailed. The human mind is often slow in accepting new ideas. The democratic process is designed to gain the opinion, knowledge, and strength of the largest number of persons possible for the support and working in the cooperative parish.

Social planning, which in our context means planning by church bodies, has been defined as a conscious process of personal interaction combining investigation, discussion, agreement, and action in order to achieve those conditions, relationships, and values regarded as desirable.[1]

If the above framework is kept in mind, several actual examples of the process by which cooperative parishes were born are related. In each case it will be noted that some of the steps in the model for a framework of social action were followed.

The Process of Consolidating or Merging Churches

In a Methodist Annual Conference in Illinois six projects of consolidation or merger of from two to four churches each were accomplished. Basic policies or ideals were established by the Board of Missions which involved: (1) a Sunday morning service of worship each Sunday; (2) a full-time minister living on the charge; (3) an adequate workload for a minister, defined as a minimum of four hundred members; (4) an adequate church program which is capable of drawing people to the church from a radius of three to ten miles; (5) an adequate salary for the minister with travel funds and other considerations. The conference missionary secretary, a full-time officer, was authorized to assist in bringing about consolidations or mergers.

The plan for consolidation consisted of the following steps: (1) A research study of the anticipated churches to merge. The study was done through the use of a self-study guide or questionnaire by each congregation. The research included the preparation of a parish map locating each participating church family, church, and other pertinent factors. (2) The recommendation for consolidation or merger was presented to the local congregation for consideration. (3) A joint planning committee was appointed for the purpose of examining further the matter of consolidation and formulating recommendations to be presented to each local church official board, quarterly conference, and to a congregational meeting. The basic committee consisted of ten to twelve persons. Subcommittees were appointed in three areas of concern: (a) one to examine the question: Where and when do we merge? (b) one to examine the question: What will this do for us? (c) one to answer the question: How much will this cost us?

Many months were taken in each case for the planning process. If recommendations to merge were received from two or more churches, a planning committee was elected to finalize such plans as building additions or a new building including location, nomination of officers, and recommendation for a name. All processes involved the conference missionary secretary and the district superintendent.

A study of the merged churches after a reasonable time revealed a high degree of satisfaction among the members.

One of the most publicized accounts of church mergers is the uniting of four Protestant congregations in Schellsburg, Pennsylvania. The four-year process is too detailed to report in this writing, but the main points are mentioned.[2]

Schellsburg is a town of 288 population. It had four churches: United Church of Christ, eighty-two members; Methodist, seventy-nine members; Presbyterian, fifty-five members; and Lutheran, sixty-eight members. The Methodist Church building had burned several years before, and the congregation rented the Presbyterian building. No congregation had a resident pastor, and each shared a minister with other congregations. Each congregation held services every other week. The Lutheran Church owned a parsonage which was rented.

Discussions for some type of church union were stimulated by executives of the Pennsylvania Council of Churches and the county Council of Churches. Denominational representatives of each of the four churches and the pastors of the local congregations were brought together in January, 1961, to discuss the future of the religious situation in the community. In April, 1961, a meeting was held in the United Church of Christ (at that time Evangelical and Reformed) with all persons of the community invited. A representative of the state Council of Churches presided, and a free discussion was entered into by laity, clergy, and denominational representatives. On March 4, 1962, representatives from the four official boards of the four churches and denominational representatives met to discuss further plans. The representatives were asked to secure from their respective congregations a vote or official action to appoint a negotiating committee to plan some form of constructive work for the churches of Schellsburg. On May 20, 1962, congregational representatives met and reported that each congregation had voted to continue discussion. A straw vote was taken in the committee to see how each person felt about merger. It was suggested that each congregation should hold a meeting and take a straw vote about a possible merger and also to vote on the issue of what the new church should be, casting their ballot for one of the other denominations on the assumption it was natural for each denomination to want its own denomination named as the representative in the new merged church.

On July 15, 1962, the representatives met to consider the straw vote. No decisive decision could be made from the voting. The denominational representatives then suggested they present to the churches one denomination to be the new united church and have all congregations vote "yes" or "no" on it. On September 22, 1962, the denominational representatives met and decided upon the United Church of Christ. This action was reported to the committee on October 28, 1962, and it was decided the churches should take six weeks for discussion. On December 2–9, 1962, the congregations met again and voted. Ballots were opened on December 9. Only the United

Church of Christ had voted "yes" for the proposal. In March, 1963, the denominational representatives met and decided a United Church of Christ pastor would be appointed. He would then serve as supply pastor for the Methodist and Presbyterian churches. The Lutheran Church would continue with its own pastor but would continue to discuss merger. The plan was approved by each congregation in separate meetings on May 23, 1963. A joint service was held July 21, 1963, with sixty-seven members present, and at a second joint service on July 28, it was agreed that they would continue the plan with services being held in different church buildings.

On September 21, 1963, a plan of union with a trial period of two years was presented. The plan called for each church continuing with the same budget as before. Each church would continue to pay its benevolences to its denomination. The Board of Missions of the United Church of Christ would supplement the budget by $4,000. All churches agreed to the plan, and October 6, 1963, was set for the first joint service and communion. It was an outstanding day with 120 persons receiving communion and 150 persons present. The plan of union was then adopted by each church. Final plans were made on November 22, 1963, including appointing of a board of directors and a United Church of Christ pastor. Further meetings resulted in adopting the United Church of Christ building for their permanent home, moving the new pastor into the community, a recognition service for the new pastor, and the Lutheran Church deeding the parsonage property for use by the pastor. Plans were made for charter membership in the new church, and finally the formal vote for merger took place October 4, 1964. More than two

103

hundred persons attended the service. The final votes were 101 for union, twenty-five opposed, and two abstaining, with each congregation having a majority in favor of union. On November 22, 1964, a uniting service with more than three hundred in attendance was held with an impressive morning service.

The above process is quite illustrative of how change can be brought about. Basically the steps presented by Beal in his plan for social action were followed. Problems arose when proper information had not been given by use of the "diffusion set" as Beal calls them, and there was a failure in choosing a sufficiently large representation for planning at certain stages.

ESTABLISHING EXTENDED MINISTRIES

Since the extended ministry involves ordinarily one minister, or in some cases the employed staff of one church and one or more additional churches, the process of establishing such ministries is quite simple. Some actual cases are described below.

A minister was assigned to a church of approximately nine hundred members in a Missouri county seat town of eight thousand population. He learned there were two open country churches left without a pastor. He asked the denominational executive to leave the churches for a time without a pastor and to give him the opportunity to see if he could work out an arrangement to serve the churches. This was done satisfactorily for the town church and country churches. Later, a third rural congregation was organized in another rural community and served by the town pastor. The arrangement required five services each

Sunday: 9 A.M. in a country church; 10 A.M. in another country church; 11 A.M. in the town church; 6:30 P.M. in a country church; and 7:30 P.M. in the town church. Many ministers would not want this heavy a Sunday schedule. However, with only one additional church as most extended ministries call for, the schedule would be less exacting. Incidentally, the extended ministry above was established in 1946, and the pastor remained on the charge for eighteen years. His successor of two years at this writing is continuing with the same arrangement, and all churches seem satisfied with the pastoral services received.

A congregation in a village of some two hundred population was without a pastor. The congregation voted to have representatives from the church approach the town church minister about serving them. The town in Nebraska has about ten thousand population, and the town church has about two thousand members. The pastor received the committee from the country church and agreed he would attempt to work out some kind of arrangement with the employed staff of the church. This was done by a plan which made it possible for one of the associate pastors to go to the village church each Sunday to lead the congregation in worship. The members of the church staff feel it is more satisfactory for the associates to be conducting services in other churches than to be performing minor roles in the town church. The extended ministry has now included two other country churches and has been developed into a larger parish. One of the associate pastors is the director of the campus ministry at a state university in the town. He directs a service each Sunday in one of the country churches since he does not have a Sunday responsibility in his campus ministry. (Incidentally, I have discovered four similar situations in which campus ministers are serving churches in open country or villages. In each case the minister uses pretheological students to assist him in his work.)

THE YOKED FIELD

Yoked fields consist of two or more churches of different denominations which are yoked together under the direction of one minister.

The "yoking" process calls for action on the part of laymen, any ministers of the denominations involved, and denominational executives.

In a New Hampshire community in 1957 the church people became alarmed over the rising rate of delinquency among the youth. It was that issue which brought together leaders from four Protestant churches to discuss what measures could be taken to reduce the delinquency rate. The churches were Episcopal, Northern Baptist, Congregational, and Methodist. Each church was small and had for a minister either a retired pastor or the part-time services of a pastor.

Out of the discussions came a proposal whereby an association of churches would be formed and one minister employed to serve all congregations. The Methodist church did not enter into the association, leaving the Episcopal, Baptist, and Congregational churches. An Episcopal minister was employed, and service schedules were agreed upon. Joint services are held on Christmas Eve in the Episcopal church, Thanksgiving Eve services are held in the Congregational church, and a three-hour Good Friday service is held in the Baptist church.

Each church maintains its own denominational identity and complete local church organization. The pastor feels this requires a great deal of his time in administrative work in keeping up with three denominational programs. A second problem faced is that of denominational polity regarding the ministry in the Episcopal church. Only a priest can administer Holy Communion. This means that if the association should employ a minister of another denomination, there would have to be a visiting priest to celebrate the sacrament of Holy Communion in the Episcopal church. Some of the Episcopal ministers are attempting to effect a denominational policy, making it possible for a minister of another denomination to have clergy recognition to administer Holy Communion in an Episcopal church in a yoked field situation. The advantages of the yoked field arrangement, however, far outweigh the disadvantages.

THE LARGER PARISH OR GROUP MINISTRY

The process by which a larger parish or group ministry is brought into being is the same as with other cooperative parishes, but generally involves more people and more congregations.

In a small city and its surrounding area on Vancouver Island, British Columbia, Canada, there were three United Church of Canada congregations, an American Indian Church, and a Chinese-speaking congregation. Some laymen in the largest of the congregations became concerned over the fact that they felt they were not making an ade-

quate witness in the area to the Christian faith. One layman in particular stimulated the thinking of others. In
the church a "Vision Committee" was appointed to study
ministry needs and renewal needs. The committee's study
included a population analysis of the area including pre-
dictions, the existing churches with their past perfor-
mances and prospective areas of service, and the existing
ministries.

Proposals were then made to the presbytery executive
for a larger parish structure with a team ministry. The
idea of the new charge arrangement was conceived in the
fall of 1965. Discussions were held among the laymen,
ministers, and the presbytery executive which led to a
combined meeting of the official boards. The matter was
then referred back to the congregations. Each local church
official board then adopted the plan.

The plan called for the appointing of three ministers
on an equal basis, a full-time worker (woman), and employment of a full-time secretary. One church, the Chinese-
speaking church, was remodeled to house the offices of the
staff. The parish actually got under way in the fall of
1966. The three basic factors in the process were origina-
tion of the idea by a group of laymen; discussion within
the congregation, between the ministers, and among denominational executives; and final adoption of the basic
ideas by all congregations.

A Nebraska district superintendent in The Methodist
Church has been quite successful in establishing several
larger parishes and group ministries. His procedure is as
follows: (1) analyze the area in which it appears a cooperative parish may prove to be an effective means of
ministering to the total area; (2) discuss the possibilities

with the ministers; (3) ask each church to appoint three persons to meet once a month over a period of one year to discuss the possibilities of the parish; (4) ask each person to read literature in the field along with the basic book (*The Cooperative Parish in Nonmetropolitan Areas*); (5) after each meeting of the lay representatives ask them to go back to their church and make a "progress report" to the official board. After the board has heard and discussed the report, they are asked to vote to continue or discontinue the discussions; (6) after a full year of the discussion, feedback, and approval process, joint meetings of congregations and official boards should be held with final approval for the plan adopted.

It can be seen in the above plan that all of the suggestions made in the first part of this chapter concerning the process of social change are used.

Parish Development Aids

Experience has proved that where sound principles of teaching, research, and open democratic procedures have been followed, it has been possible to bring into being an effective cooperative parish with a minimum of friction or loss of support and a maximum amount of cooperation. It is a process, a time-consuming process, which must involve denominational executives, ministers, and laymen.

In Appendix C of this volume will be found a guide for a six-session course to assist laymen and pastors in understanding the basic factors in developing, organizing, and putting into operation a cooperative parish. This volume is suggested as a basic text to be used by all persons engaged in the study. The author is convinced after many years of working in a cooperative parish, studying scores of parishes, and assisting in establishing many parishes, that by following sound leadership principles and using a study guide as is here suggested, a parish can be brought into being with full support of the laymen and a saving of many months of time.

CHAPTER V

The Cooperative Parish at Work

The cooperative parish is designed to assist the members of local congregations to be the church at worship, nurture, and work. Therefore, the task of the cooperative parish is no different from that of a local congregation, but is designed to assist a local congregation to do a better task of being the church. One of the tragedies of the contemporary church is its limitation in areas of service within the world. Congregations become ingrown and self-satisfied without any feeling of a need for expansion in a greater fulfillment of the task of mission in the world. The cooperative parish offers many opportunities for creative means of witnessing to the Word in the world.

THE COUNCIL

Cooperative parishes need to have a council composed of representatives from each congregation. The number of representatives will be determined by the size of the parish and number of congregations. Ordinarily, there are from one to three persons elected from each local congregation to serve on the parish council. The parish council becomes the major planning body for the activities of the total parish. The council will meet periodically to plan the total activities for the parish involved. Generally, once each month or each quarter is adequate depending upon the size of the parish. The council needs to make serious study of the needs within the local area. One of the valuable lessons taught by the inner city missions of the last ten to fifteen years has been that the mission will start with the immediate needs of the people in the area. Frequently, the needs are economic and for better health measures; thus, the parish begins by attempting to meet such physical needs. The program then expands to the development of the religious life of the people involved and eventually into a more crystallized form of church organization. In most of our nonmetropolitan areas existing churches come together to form cooperative parishes, and the needs are primarily those of ministering within a congregation which already exists. The congregation then will begin to examine the needs of the local area and take constructive measures to minister to those needs.

The parish council will need subcommittees responsible for the various activities of the parish which are reflected through the work of local congregations. Most denominations have programs which center within six major areas:

evangelism, mission, education, Christian social concern, worship, and stewardship. Some denominations may have as many as ten or twelve committees, and others may have less than the six major areas listed. Nevertheless, study has revealed that the six basic areas will cover almost every phase of activity and concern of a local church. Within the parish council subcommittees should be established for each of the six basic areas with responsibility for assisting local congregations and the parish at large in fulfilling the mission of the church. In addition, there will need to be subcommittees for women's work, men's work, and youth activities. The nine committees will generally be sufficient to meet the total needs of the parish.

The committees of the council need ample opportunity for reporting at various council meetings and also for bringing to the council in a detailed form the interest of the total parish within their field. The various committees should have authority to move into local congregations in assisting them to implement their work around the committee's interest.

On occasion there will need to be special committees appointed to look after certain interests of the parish such as charge boundaries, church location and cooperation, farm and home interests, cooperation with community agencies, lay speakers, and special parish events.

The most active persons within each local congregation need to be elected to the parish council, and the strongest leadership of the parish should be the officers of the council.

The executive committee, usually consisting of the elected officers of the council, needs to meet on occasion with the employed staff of the cooperative parish to keep the coordinated program alive and effective. The members of the employed staff are ex officio members of the council and as such are to be present at each meeting and have the right of the floor and vote. Strong lines of communication should be maintained at all times between the council, the employed staff, and each local congregation.

FINANCING THE COOPERATIVE PARISH

The type of financial program for a cooperative parish is dependent upon the type of parish involved. If the parish consists of one rural community (locality group II) which is a town with its surrounding rural neighborhoods (locality group I) , it is possible to have a completely unified budget. In this case the parish council will draw up a budget consisting of staff salaries, the denominational executive's salary, connectional items for the denomination or denominations, mission giving, and any other item which affects the total parish. Allowances need to be made for staff travel, office expense, the parish paper, and special parish events. Each church within the parish will accept its proportionate share of the budget and pay to a common treasurer who in turn will make all payments for the parish. Each local congregation will need a treasurer who will receive funds from the members of the church through their regular contributions. He will make the payments for the congregation through the parish treasurer. Each local congregation will take care of its church school literature, building maintenance, custodial services, and utilities. The unified budget described above has been found to operate very successfully in many cooperative parishes. The unified budget will operate quite effectively in the extended ministry, enlarged charge, larger parish, or yoked field.

In the group ministry support of individual staff members, with the exception of a specialized worker who serves the whole area, should come from the charge served by the individual pastor. Each pastor in the group ministry serves one or more congregations. This is his definite responsibility, and he should receive his salary from the churches he serves. In this event, the group ministry as such does not have a large central treasury. It will need to have a treasurer who will receive funds from each church to support enterprises involving all of the churches. Supported from the central fund are such items as a parish paper, office expenses for the director, an annual parish day, and other cooperative activities. If there is a specialist who serves the total area, such as a rural worker, her salary and travel expenses should be paid through the common fund. The group ministry ordinarily is operated in the enlarged community (locality group III) where ties are not strong enough for a program of closely integrated operation, such as the larger parish.

Treasurers need to keep very accurate records of all receipts and disbursements, and books should be available for examination by any person or group within the parish. An annual audit needs to be made by impersonal auditors and a report made to the parish council which should also be published in some kind of parish-wide circular.

COOPERATIVE ACTIVITIES OF A PARISH

There are many areas of cooperation involving all of the churches within a parish. The ingenuity of the group in planning can discover areas that are beyond this discussion.

The parish paper. An essential in any kind of cooperative ministry is some type of parish paper which can take the form of a mimeographed page or a rather elaborate, printed magazine-type of publication. Regardless of the actual form, there are several underlying principles which need to be observed:

1. The paper should not be on a subscription basis. Support should come from the cooperating churches on the basis of the number of families in the church. If there is no central treasury from which such a paper can be supported, it would need to be supported by the local churches involved. This support could come from an amount set aside in the church budget, from the church school, or from individual contributions. The paper will be defeated in its purpose if subscriptions are taken. Any subscription paper will not go to all families. The paper should also be mailed to all constituents of the church in the parish as a means of cultivating prospects for parish membership. Support is not difficult to obtain after the paper has had two or three issues.

2. The paper needs to be mailed from one central office to all families within the membership of the churches of the parish. It needs to be mailed to all prospective families for church membership. Such a list of prospects can be compiled by careful examination of church school records, youth activity rolls, women's society rolls, and lists of persons contacted in any organization within the church. Additional members of families who are not members of the church will be discovered. Visitation cards should be carefully kept for persons visiting in

church services. The community house-to-house survey is a source of discovering membership prospects. Any family contacted in any way by the church or any family without a church home becomes a potential for church membership. These persons need to receive the parish paper.

3. The paper needs to have a standing column which announces the church service schedule for all congregations, names and addresses of staff members, ministers, and members of the lay council.

4. The paper should carry articles of general concern to the entire area. It needs to be used as a means of announcing events involving all churches and reports of events which have taken place. A column needs to be devoted to the activities of each church, using the names of persons freely in reporting local church activities. Space should be given to denominational programs of general, churchwide nature. Many readers will not receive the church organ of the denomination, and the parish paper can provide a limited amount of general information. There needs to be a calendar of events and announcements. Articles on timely topics by members of the staff need to be published, but sermons, generally, are not very interesting reading.

5. Someone within the parish—a minister, the director, or a layman—should be appointed by the council to be the editor of the paper. The best talent available needs to be secured for this task. It does take time, but it is one of the efforts that will pay large dividends when well done. The usual news formula of who, when, where, what, and why can be applied to preparing news articles. News is a reporting of incidents that people will find interesting.

6. The mechanics of preparing and distributing the paper must be assigned to some person or persons designated by the council. A good mimeograph production has advantages of being more inexpensive than printing. Stress, however, should be placed on *quality*. Care needs to be taken in preparing stencils, the use of the heavy paper, proper ink, and uniform distribution of ink. Contemporary offset types of printing will produce a nicer paper than mimeograph at a relatively inexpensive cost. Frequently a small town printer will prepare the paper in printed form for only a little more cost than mimeographing. Much more material can go into a printed paper than a mimeographed one. Sixteen pages of double-spaced typed material can be put into four pages of printed matter the same size. Printing and offset have the added advantage of the use of pictures.

The person responsible for circulating the paper must have resources available for keeping an up-to-date mailing list. This needs to be revised constantly through the assistance of staff members. Some type of addressing machine should be supplied by the council. Mailing can be done with a special postal law regulation permit for nonprofit organizations which provide mailing at a minimum cost per copy.

Activity groups in the parish. There are three main activity groups within the structure of the organized church: youth, men, and women. As far as possible, each of these groups needs to be recognized in planning the overall program of the cooperative parish. If the parish is denominational, the program of the denomination should be used. If interdenominational, the program can assist greatly in interest for the entire area and stimulate a stronger program in the local church.

There should be a youth organization consisting of all young people from each local church. This cannot, except in the case of a very small parish, take the place of local church organizations. Young people enjoy the fellowship of other young people. They enjoy "going places" and will go places when left on their own. A monthly parish meeting of the young people, consisting of periods of worship, study, and recreation, will create interest and strengthen the entire Christian cause. Once each year the youth from all churches need to have a prolonged program covering the greater part of three days. Such a program can be in the winter; the young people can meet at the sponsoring church beginning with the evening meal on Friday, continue through Saturday, and close with the noon meal on Sunday. The program for such a meeting must be well balanced between worship opportunities, study classes on timely topics, and recreation. The sponsoring church can entertain the young people in homes overnight and through breakfast. Other meals can be provided by the women's society. A small fee can be charged to take care of expense. When church building facilities are not adequate, frequently the high school building can be used. The members of the parish staff can be used as speakers, teachers, and recreation leaders. The denominational personnel from connectional offices will be happy to give leadership in such an endeavor.

A strong program of summer camping ought to be promoted for youth in the parish. Young people can attend their denominational camps, but emphasis can be placed upon the camp by the entire group.

119

The work of the men can be greatly enhanced by periodic meetings of all men from the cooperating churches. These meetings can be held at different churches at stated times. There should be some type of organization of the men, placing responsibility in the hands of proper persons for program and planning. Frequently the men's organization becomes the sponsoring agent for a layman's speaking group to supplement worship services in the parish and to speak in local churches on timely subjects. Fellowship can be stimulated by a men's organization, creating splendid worship and learning opportunities.

The work of the women of the parish is usually more clearly defined by denominational women's societies than that of the men. Many small congregations, however, find the denominational organization too complicated to follow. It is difficult to have an active society with five women when the organization calls for sixteen officers. Nevertheless, the five women need the fellowship and strength of the larger organization. Sometimes a small church can organize as a circle of a larger church not too far away. Certain activities can be done together, such as business and study sessions or special training classes. The stronger churches can be of great assistance to the smaller churches.

Leadership education. The cry from churches across the nation is constantly for more and better-trained church school leaders and teachers. The cooperative parish provides a means for training teachers and church leaders by having annually or twice each year training classes on a parish-wide basis. It is difficult to secure teachers for leadership classes for the very small congregation, but teachers can be secured for a leadership school in which there are a number of churches cooperating. Transportation facilities make it possible for teachers to travel to such training schools several miles away. Denominational executive secretaries of education will welcome the opportunity to assist in setting up schools and providing teachers. Classes should be conducted in administration of the church school, methods of teaching children, youth, and adults, how to use literature, the Bible, church history, theology, and many other subjects relevant to the teaching-learning process.

The Parish Day. At least annually there should be a parish day, drawing all members of all congregations together for a full day of church activity. The program should be on Sunday and consist of church school for all age groups, morning worship service, a basket dinner, and an afternoon program. The observance would probably tax the capacity of the largest church building in the area and needs to be held in some type of open-air pavilion. A special lay council committee will be needed to make the plans. Such plans call for selecting church school teachers, selecting the speaker for the day, providing the facilities for the meeting, such as tables for the dinner, musical instruments, drinking water, rest rooms, parking grounds, hymnbooks, a printed order of service, the program, choirs, and persons to assist in parking cars. The speaker for the meeting should be someone brought in for the day, such as a specialist in the field of town and country work. His expenses—travel, entertainment, and an honorarium—can be provided for with the offering at the meeting.

The parish day brings a spirit of enthusiasm to the entire constituency. It gives the members of the individual churches an opportunity to meet the others in the parish and gives the parish an opportunity to express its strength. Widespread publicity will be given to such a meeting by public press. The parish witnesses as a cooperative program for the Christian cause. It makes an opportunity to bring to the area outstanding national leadership in the field of town and country church. This is not possible for a church working alone, but when resources are pooled, leaders are anxious for the opportunity to participate in such a gathering.

Cooperation with Agencies. There are many agencies working in nonmetropolitan areas for the betterment of the total community life. The county agricultural agent and his assistants, the soil conservation service, farmers' organizations, vocational home economics and agricultural departments in high schools, and other persons and organizations are working for the county. The parish staff should know leaders in various fields and be in a position to cooperate with their programs. Staff personnel of various agencies can be invited to assist in parish programs wherever they have a contribution to make.

Many cooperative parishes have done phenomenal work in regard to the various programs of private and government agencies for the relief of suffering throughout the world. For instance, a Baptist parish in Kansas sent a layman farmer to Thailand on a special mission project for the denomination. They also sponsored sending a truckload of pigs, goats, and heifers for 4-H Club members to Venezuela. Many parishes have been responsible for participation in the "Heifer for Relief" program and the "Foods for Peace" programs around the world. The anti-poverty programs of various forms, both government and privately sponsored, have been supported in various ways by parish constituents. Extensive adult education programs have been entered into by both church and community for betterment of the total life of the area. Most states have adult education programs sponsored by the extension departments of the state land grant colleges which can prove to be very beneficial and effective in local congregations.

Community organization has been one of the major concerns of some cooperative parishes. A community organization is a program whereby a local town and its surrounding area organize all the major interests and concerns of the community for betterment. The organization generally consists of representatives from each civic group, businessmen, the school system, and each of the churches represented in the community. The needs of the community are studied, and action is taken to meet those needs. Community organizations generally examine the life of the community in the following categories: health and welfare, education, recreation and leisure time, sanitation, religion, government, and a sound economic base for the community. As these areas are studied, the analysis discovers whether or not the community is meeting all the needs of the people within the area, and some means are devised to attempt to meet the deficiencies. The cooperative parish can be of great assistance in such community organization and structure.

Simultaneous Action. There is increased strength for the churches if they will do many things at the same time. Vacation church schools, evangelistic campaigns, Lord's Acre programs, visitation programs, and other activities can be strengthened if promoted in all the churches of the parish at the same dates. The staff can plan together

123

how to do the work; literature can be secured in bulk orders; publicity can be done together. The psychology of group action will strengthen the total program. If some church is reluctant to launch into some phase of the work of the church, simultaneous action by the other churches will encourage its participation.

One of the largest benefits from simultaneous action is that of advertising. Newspapers are anxious to give space to churches; however, so much material sent to the editor is simply routine announcements that he becomes weary in his effort to be of service to the church. He even looks for the opportunities to publicize any work that is on a broad scale. Publishers are concerned with material which reaches the largest number of their readers. Parish-wide programs are of concern to many people and make for good reading. The church needs to take advantage of all opportunities for good publicity.

An Active Farm and Home and a Job Committee. One of the major problems of the rural church is the depletion of population. Young people finish high school, and unable to find a position, they must migrate to the larger town or city for gainful employment. There needs to be a committee in the parish to study the "job opportunity" situation within the area. It would be well for the committee to invite the agricultural extension agent, the local bankers, leading merchants, and agricultural leaders to come together in discussion of methods of providing ways by which young people can secure adequate employment to remain in the community. The 4-H and Future Farmers programs are stimulating many youth with a desire to remain in their community. Nevertheless, confronted with the necessity of having a large cash outlay to begin farming, they find it impossible to finance the operation and must go on to the city. An active committee in the parish should plan for distribution of literature on father-son farm operating agreements, family farm transfer agreements, and on assisting young people in getting started in small businesses.[1]

Additional Areas for Ministry. The parish staff and the parish council need to make careful observations of the area in which the parish is located to discover if there are needs for special types of ministries. Many areas now are rapidly becoming predominant areas of recreation as people press out of the cities to try to find a bit of nature and to be relieved of the tensions of urban life. If a cooperative parish has within its area any kind of resort or concentration of people seeking recreation, there is a need to devise some means of ministering to such persons. Usually the most effective kind of ministry to persons in resort areas is to establish some type of cooperative interdenominational council to work out a program to meet the needs. The cooperative parish can take the initiative in beginning such council and making a careful study of what the needs are. Very effective ministries have been designed by a number of cooperative parishes in this manner.

Parish councils and parish staffs need to make careful examination of the area in which they are located to discover if there are any "isolated groups." Isolated groups are persons who are isolated because of race, nationality, ethnic background, or economic levels. Very often a whole neighborhood of persons will be ignored by the existing congregations, and for years the churches will fail to minister to a large segment of people who are socially

125

or culturally isolated. A careful study should be made of such situations, and a form of ministry needs to be planned to meet such needs. I discovered one parish in Canada in which the staff of a larger parish ministers to a group of native American Indians and also to a group of Chinese-speaking people. It is not uncommon any place in the United States for totally white congregations to be completely unaware of existing Negro congregations even of the same denomination or of large segments of Negroes who are not being served by any church. A cooperative ministry offers an excellent opportunity for cooperating with existing churches of various races and for developing a ministry for persons of different races. A larger parish in southeast Missouri which has been organized for twenty years has within the last two years incorporated two Negro congregations into it. A rule of thumb for any cooperative ministry can be to attempt to discover any needs within the parish boundaries and devise ways and means of meeting those needs.

In a day when many new and nonconventional forms of ministry are coming into existence, the cooperative parish offers many opportunities for exploration of new ideas.

For instance, most small cities of three thousand population or more have a radio broadcasting station. The cooperative parish can purchase regular time on the radio for programs which will be educational, worshipful, and stimulating to the listener. Television time is much more difficult to obtain, but television stations are glad to include good news items in broadcasts. Many cooperative parishes have a good story to tell and need to get it on the air.

126

Open-air services for summer evangelism can be sponsored. The use of a drive-in theater, a tent, or public park facility can be sponsored by a cooperative parish. Too often the work of the church is confined to the church building.

Telephone ministries have been effective in some areas. Persons are trained to do calling by phone for survey of church participation and also for publicizing the church. In some cases persons are trained to be "counselors by phone," and a group of persons are ready at all times to receive phone calls to assist any person in need. This is a large program which requires much study and preparation.

The Christian ministry has traditionally filled a large role in the field of personal counseling. Special training in the field is now offered in seminaries, and many ministers are more skilled than ever before. The public needs to be informed of this fact and specific plans made for counseling to take place. I discovered a larger parish in Canada in which rooms were designed in the central church to provide space for each minister on the staff for use in counseling sessions.

One parish in Montana is considering sponsoring a "restaurant church." This would be across the street from the public high school and would provide a place for young people to go for wholesome associations. It would also stress families eating together. At a stated time each evening a brief service of worship would be conducted by one of the staff members. The waiters and waitresses would be trained as counselors and would be free to counsel with persons who indicate a need for counsel.

One cooperative parish in a lake resort area displayed

127

Christian art in a large building. There were times for showing films, and persons were available for discussion and counseling. A small card was distributed in public places which read:

Visit the Treasure House for Living. See the festival of Christianity and the arts—including sculpture, paintings, photography, and art objects from across the nation. Ask to see the film "The Parable" made famous at the New York World's Fair. Secure free tickets for the Vesper Cruise leaving Loc-wood dock each Sunday evening at 7:30 on the *Tom Sawyer*. Located adjacent to Loc-wood dock at the dam.

During the course of the summer thousands of persons visited the Treasure House, and there was always a waiting list for the Vesper Cruise on the excursion boat. This same parish is considering an open-air drama of religious nature for the next summer.

The opportunities in the contemporary church for witnessing in new forms of ministry are many. An ingenious staff and creative parish council can perform many services by thinking together and giving the Holy Spirit an opportunity to be released in the world.

Goals for Cooperative Parishes. The parish council needs to think through the objectives of a cooperative program. It is always a good policy to have standards toward which the group is moving. A list of goals is given below as suggestions.

1. Worship services in each church at least once each Sunday.
2. Vacation church school in each church annually.
3. At least annual opportunities for teacher training.

128

4. A program of missionary education in each church, using missionary speakers, visual aids, and classes.
5. All youth active in their local church and parish programs, summer camps, and midwinter institutes.
6. All women of the parish having an opportunity to participate in a women's organization.
7. An active men's program for all men of the parish.
8. A strong stewardship program that makes it possible for the parish to support itself and carry a proportional share of mission work.
9. A constructive program of education, visitation, and mass evangelism in every church.
10. The efficient use of such media as newspapers, radio, and television.
11. Cooperation with agricultural agencies in the area.
12. Creation of new forms of ministry to serve as many people as possible.

CONCLUSIONS

A concluding word needs to be said about the cooperative parish. All churches should feel the total responsibility for the work of the whole area involved. Harlow S. Mills was right in his diagnosis of the work of a larger parish. His criteria are repeated for emphasis.

1. The real objective of the church is to serve people, and its claim for support rests upon the same ground upon which every other institution bases its claim for support—that is, it gives value received.
2. The church must serve *all* the people within the parish area.

3. [The church] must serve *all* the interests of the people.

4. The village church, if it would fulfill its mission, must be responsible for the country evangelization.

5. If the village church would fulfill its mission, it must be a community church.[2]

By a group of churches looking seriously at the task of ministering to all of the people and all of the needs of the people within their area, a strong church program can be effected.

Such a cooperative endeavor has brought a spirit of optimism to the discouraged church. Members of a small congregation sense the strength of the whole group; they feel they are not alone and have a mission to perform. As the churches in a cooperative parish become stronger in every way, they become more attractive to the person who is unchurched, and thus, they are able to do a better task of evangelism.

The leadership of a parish must always keep in mind the goals and work of the church in the whole area— a group of ministers and congregations working together to minister effectively and efficiently to the total constituency of the community.

CHAPTER VI

Leadership
in a Cooperative Parish

In any type of cooperative parish where two or more persons are employed to be leaders, there are many opportunities for human encounters and difficulties. It is not within the scope of this chapter to make a detailed analysis of human relations and leadership techniques, but a few fundamental principles of leadership are presented. Experience has shown that an employed staff enters into a cooperative parish with high hopes, dreams, and an enthusiastic zeal. Frequently as the "new wears off" and the accomplishments are not as great as anticipated, interpersonal frictions arise between staff members. The questions of why frictions occur and what can be done about them are then raised.

Preventive measures are better than curative medicines.

Parish councils, denominational executives, official boards, and staff personnel will do well to study fundamental qualities of human relations for employed staff. Some of these qualities are discussed below.

STAFF CONSIDERATIONS

1. *Salary arrangements.* "Fair pay" is far more important than just "good pay." Employment satisfaction is dependent upon whether or not the employee feels he has been treated fairly in the light of peers in the same general age and position brackets. Church officials need to study salary arrangements for persons in similar positions, persons with similar education and experience, and persons with comparable positions in urban church employment.

Salaries for all members of the staff should be examined in the light of responsibilities, ages, experience, and family responsibilities. Too large a salary differential in a staff can be grounds for much unhappiness. Some staffs solve the problem by establishing an equal salary base with compensation for family size.

2. *Housing.* It is customary within Christendom to supply housing for the minister. This is recognized by the federal government in that house rent and monetary housing allowance are nontaxable. Fairly equal housing needs to be provided for all members of the staff. The customs of the denominations cooperating should be taken into account.

3. *Retirement plans.* All members of the staff need to be provided with some type of retirement plan. Most denominations have retirement plans for ordained clergy.

The unordained member of the staff is often forgotten, however. Denominations usually have some plan whereby unordained church employees can come under their retirement plan. Social Security is now available for all nonordained employees on the institutional-share basis. Ordained clergy, however, must carry their own Social Security as self-employed. A local congregation or a parish organization must elect to place its employees on Social Security.

4. *Travel.* All persons employed must have an adequate travel allowance. The demands for pastoral services require much travel. Parish councils or official boards should make a fair allowance for travel. One parish staff is allowed five hundred dollars a year per staff person "for the car" and an additional five cents per mile. The five hundred dollars is for insurance and a "nest egg" to purchase the next car. The five cents per mile is for fuel and upkeep. The staff members are quite happy with the arrangement.

5. *A system of salary advancement.* Some system of regular increases in salaries needs to be established. Advancements should be made on the basis of experience, years of service, and the general economic trend.

6. *Stated vacation and leave time.* Each member of the staff ought to be given an annual vacation with pay. This will vary with denominations and customs. Some form of "sabbatical leave" needs to be established so that an extended time every three to six years can be arranged, giving staff members three to six months for travel or study.

All of the above arrangements need to be put in writing by the parish council or official board. Much misunderstanding can be avoided if the above suggestions are adhered to.

7. *A job description.* A job description is a written statement which defines areas of work and responsibilities. There needs to be a job description for each employed member of the staff. Basically the job description assists the individual in understanding his own position and his relationship with other employed members of the staff. It helps the congregation or cooperating congregations to understand the duties, functions, and responsibilities of the members of the staff. A job description should be reviewed every six months to a year in a new organization and revised as needs arise. It should be considered as descriptive rather than as a legally binding document.

The job description needs to contain the following elements: (1) statement of title of position; (2) lines of responsibility, e.g., to whom the party is responsible for reporting, advice, guidance, complaints, or requests; (3) a statement of duties and responsibilities; (4) a (flexible) schedule of work time; (5) vacation periods, days off, and holidays to be observed; (6) salary, retirement benefits, expense accounts, and other considerations; (7) opportunities for self-improvement; and (8) advancements.

In a cooperative parish the congregations should be informed through a brief, concise publication about the members of the staff and the responsibilities of each person on the staff. The people need to know to whom they can look for their pastoral needs, who will be conducting services of worship in their church, and who is responsible for the various activities of the parish. Much confusion can be avoided if good job descriptions are prepared and followed.

134

8. *The staff meeting.* Staff meetings will consist of all employed persons in the cooperative parish and the regional denominational executives. Meetings should be held regularly and at a stated time—in a closely integrated cooperative parish, once a week. In a loosely integrated cooperative parish once or twice a month will be often enough.

There are three main types of staff meetings: (1) fellowship; (2) business; (3) study and personal enrichment.

The *fellowship meeting* is placed first, not by accident, but in order of importance. Fellowship is the basis for human relations, and out of it will grow understanding, love, and a sense of oneness in task and purpose. At least monthly the staff, including all members of the families, needs to get together for a "covered dish" meal and fellowship. The pastorate or work in a staff in nonmetropolitan areas is generally a lonely position. Workers are isolated from fellow workers. Family gatherings assist greatly in supplying the need for human association. Wives of staff members are an integral part of the leadership of the parish and need to be part of the fellowship and, to a degree, engage in planning the work.

Differences among the staff members and wives in education, cultural background, and theological positions are minimized around the fellowship table. Jesus was using good psychology when he frequently broke bread together with his disciples.

The *business sessions* should be conducted with sincerity, earnestness, and in an atmosphere of democracy. A definite time of meeting ought to be set with outside limits of time for closing the meeting. An agenda should be prepared by the presiding officer with ample opportunity for additional items of business to be presented by other staff members. The agenda needs to include preaching schedules, lay speaker's schedules, special events, routine emphasis upon the programs of the local church, seasonal emphasis, denominational programs, connectional meetings, committee reports, vacation church schools, special programs of evangelism, stewardship activities, and so forth.

A third type of meeting held by the staff is for the purpose of *study and personal enrichment*. All professional churchmen should keep abreast of what is taking place in the various academic fields related to the ministry. One of the tragedies of the contemporary ministry is that the demands of the day-by-day administrative and pastoral duties become so great that the minister neglects his study and sermon preparation. Stated times need to be set aside for the staff to get together for study. For instance, the stimulation of a group participating in simultaneous examination of a bit of literature can be fruitful. Some book on the Bible, theology, Christian ethics, church history, missions, or other related fields can be the basis of such a study, with each member of the staff accepting the responsibility for leading the discussion. Most seminaries now have extensive programs of continuing education which may fit quite well into the study program of a parish staff.

Early in the development of a cooperative parish the staff should try to define basic aims, goals, and objectives of the cooperative parish. This will call for extensive discussion and a final articulation in writing of what it is hoped will be accomplished by the staff in the parish. Much confusion can be avoided if all the staff understand what the basic objectives of the cooperative parish are. Such objectives need to be condensed into a few sentences and given wide publicity in the parish.

RELATIONSHIPS WITH LEADERSHIP GROUPS

A leadership group is any group within the parish which has leadership responsibility. Three main groups exist within most cooperative staff structures: (1) the employed staff; (2) the parish council; and (3) the official board of each congregation. Each of the above groups needs to possess a sense of autonomy, but at the heart of the work of each group is cooperation with every other group.

1. *The employed staff.* Parish staffs are in a position to direct the work of the parish, but at all times should keep in mind that they are the servants of the congregation. The church is the laity, and the task of the staff is to help the laity be the church! Too often members of the staff become over-anxious and over-zealous in their desire to see the work of the parish develop and move ahead of the laity rather than develop lay leadership.

2. *The council.* In a cooperative parish there should be a council composed of representatives from each congregation. The members of the staff are ex officio members of the council. The primary purpose of the council is to be the initiator and promoter of the total program of the parish. In some situations the council will be responsible for selecting and employing staff.

The members of the council need to take their work seriously. They represent their local congregation and should at all times be in a position to take back to the local congregation the plans of the staff council and the parish staff, and to express personal opinions in group meetings and speak for the church.

The council must be creative in thinking with the other members and the staff in developing a program for the group of churches working in cooperation. Harmony will prevail if each member will do his work with sincerity to the best of his ability.

The chairman of the council is the presiding officer at all meetings. He should have a carefully prepared agenda and keep the business sessions moving orderly and on schedule. At all times the chairman needs to be in close touch with the director of the parish and members of the staff.

Numerous committees should be appointed within the staff. Ample opportunity needs to be provided in council meetings for committee reports.

3. *The official board.* (The term is used to represent the official body of a local church such as board of deacons, elders, presbyters, stewards, or whatever applies in the particular denomination.) The purpose of a cooperative parish is to strengthen individual persons in each congregation. In other words, one of the major tasks of the cooperative parish is to assist each local congregation to be a better witness within its own membership and to the world. The official board should assist the congregation in being loyal to the parish program. If there is a constitution in the parish, it should be reviewed periodically. Official boards need to assist the congregation in interpreting the constitution and to bear the sentiments of the congregation to the parish council. Representatives from the local congregation on the parish council must have ample opportunity to report the actions of the council

in board meetings. Dates for council activities should be cleared, proposed programs presented, reports of parish activities made. At times the board must report to the congregation in Sunday church school and services of worship with regard to the work of the parish. It is essential that clear channels of communication be maintained between the council, the parish staff, the official board, and the congregation. The official board can serve as a liaison between these groups.

A fourth position of leadership needs to be kept in mind. That is the *denominational executive officer*. Most denominations have field representatives who are assigned to a geographic region and who are responsible for assisting the congregations in the region. The area may be known as a synod, district, county, state, or other region. The work of the executive may vary greatly from purely advisory to administrative. In every case, however, the denominational representative is a valuable person to assist in establishing and maintaining cooperative parishes. On occasion he may be able to provide the basic research necessary in the early stages of a parish and may be in a position to inform congregations of the meaning of a parish and advantages which will come from the organization. Many times the denominational representative can be the person who brings a cooperative parish into existence. He is the "professional assistant" who can direct the entire organizational process.

It is often the denominational representative to whom the council will turn for suggestions regarding the staff. He is responsible for maintaining top quality leadership in the parish and must assist the parish when a change of leadership is necessary. He is the liaison person between the parish, parish leadership, and the denominational connectional organization.

SOME QUALIFICATIONS OF A DIRECTOR
OF A COOPERATIVE PARISH

The success or failure of a cooperative program is dependent, to a large degree, upon the qualifications of the director for his position. A director's role is not easy. He must have the ability to lead others without the authority of a superior office; he must have an understanding of human nature to the degree of ability to cope with the differences of personality characteristics, educational qualifications, theological prejudices and interpretations, and the psychological makeup of individuals in the staff. Four main qualifications of the director are presented for consideration on the part of one who is considering being a director and to assist those persons who are seeking a director for a parish: (1) an appreciation of rural life; (2) a consecration to the task of service in the rural church; (3) a knowledge of rural social systems and rural sociology; and (4) an understanding of basic leadership procedures.

1. *An appreciation of rural life.* A director must be in sympathy with rural life, feeling that there is a definite contribution rural people make to the total culture. One of the basic theories of sociology is that there is always a tendency for urban culture to dominate the total thinking of a people and that rural life is minimized in importance. This is reflected in the fact that there is always a migration of population from rural to urban areas except in time of catastrophe, such as war or famine. The bright lights

140

of the city attract the attention of the nation. There is a premium placed upon the professional man who makes a success of his work in the city—doctor, lawyer, teacher, minister. One who does a successful work in a rural area is seldom recognized until he has had the stamp of approval placed upon him by the city. A parish director must be mindful of these facts. He must be willing to work in the framework of this knowledge, accepting the role for the merits in the case. These merits are legion. The parish director must feel his task is important in the whole economy of the nation, important in his denomination and in the universal church.

If a director feels his task is simply to use the position as a stepping-stone to a better position or a more prominent one in his church, he had better refuse the position. He should feel that this task is one of the most important positions in the church.

2. Closely related to the sense of appreciation of rural life is that of a *consecration to the task of service in the rural church*. With a shortage of qualified ministerial leadership in most of the leading denominations of the nation and the glamour of a rapidly growing urban culture with all the opportunities for the establishment of new churches, it is easy for one to lose his sense of mission to rural America. The Protestant churches do not recognize the rural pastorate in equal proportion to the urban, or even with equal proportion to the missionary who serves in a faraway land. There is the feeling that the minister who remains in a rural pastorate or leadership in the rural church somehow could not prove himself a capable leader for a larger responsibility. This is a phenomenon with which a parish director must reckon. He

must be willing to face this fact, knowing full well certain recognitions will probably never come his way which do come to some ministers in his denomination. A sense of mission, a sense of calling, however, has always marked the prophet, and he has been willing, without complaint or defensiveness, to continue his work in the light of a task to be done. The director must live in a constant state of consecration—as should all ministers for that matter—holding the basic elements of the gospel ministry uppermost in his mind. It is helpful to keep in one's thinking the statements of Christ: "Even the Son of man came not to be ministered unto, but to minister"; "The servant is not greater than his lord"; "He that is greatest among you, let him be your servant."

3. *A knowledge of rural social systems and rural sociology* is important to the parish director. There was a time when it was felt that a rural minister should be well-versed in agriculture so that he could, to a certain degree, serve as an agricultural consultant. In a day of specialization, when there are from one to ten full-time employed agricultural specialists in most counties in America and when theological training is a long and tedious process, the minister does not have time to train in agriculture, nor is there the need for it. He needs, however, to have enough training in modern agricultural methods to appreciate them and to guide the farmer within his parish to the specialist within his county. He needs to know how to work with the agricultural extension agent, the vocational agricultural teacher, the soil conservationist. He ought to be acquainted with the services available from the agricultural college within the state. His parish can be a means of contact for various

social and agricultural agencies. This means the director must know the people who are working in his county and must have a close working relationship with them. He can be a member of farmers' organizations in the area, provided he can agree with their policies. They can be of assistance to his people, and he can be of assistance to them.

The director should have enough work in rural sociology and rural church administration to understand something of the nature of rural society. This will facilitate his getting along with people and his appreciation of the unseen forces which influence the minds of rural people. Group solidarity, intimacy of kin, clannishness, slowness in acceptance of new ideas, a reverence of tradition—all are marks of rural culture. The parish leader will recognize these and adjust his work to fit them rather than oppose them. If a director has not had the opportunity to study rural sociology formally, he should arrange for short courses or additional seminary work or courses in a department of sociology in a college or university. Constant reading in the field assists in keeping one abreast of scholarly developments.

4. *An understanding of leadership procedures.* The field of leadership as a study is comparatively new. Literature is being produced by sociologists, business and church administrators, and psychologists, which now has made available many books and periodicals in the field.

The director must be able to get along with people. In the church there are a few situations in which a minister is in authority over another minister. In the episcopal form of government, certain officials—district superintendent and bishop—are delegated such authoritative positions, but a minister, though he may be a parish director, is still a minister among many. For this reason, the parish director must understand fully democratic leadership methods. He must be capable of throwing himself fully into the democratic process of group procedure, realizing that true democracy in group action is the most permanent form of group control. He must be winsome in personality, sincere in his motives, and have the ability to share with the ministers in the parish successes and failures. Precept and example are the best rules to follow. A task well done in his own responsibilities will speak loudly to the other ministers on the staff. A fellowship of the ministers, which emerges through informal group gatherings, frequent family dinners, occasional parties and picnics, will go a long way in breaking down any barriers between members of the staff.

One of the problems faced in a parish staff is the diversity in training of the ministers. Because of a shortage of ministers in many denominations, hundreds of men and women are being used as pastors who have not had the advantage of formal education for the ministry. There is a tendency on the part of the untrained to hold rather dogmatic ideas on theological beliefs which are defended with great emotion, and to feel that the trained person has "lost his passion" for the gospel. This makes for a decided barrier between the director and some members of the staff. Such barriers can be overcome with profound appreciation on the part of the director for the untrained minister who, in his own right, has a genuine call to the Christian ministry and a sincere desire to serve the church. Humility on the part of the director, appreciation for others, and a recognition of the contribution every person on the staff can make to the thinking of the group will aid in overcoming barriers of difference in education. Too much cannot be said regarding the necessity of a director to be brotherly, sincere, and honest in every respect in his work with the members of the staff.

As equally difficult as the problems that arise with the untrained minister are the problems that may arise with the newly graduated seminarian. Frequently the young minister is assigned or elected to a position in a cooperative parish without understanding the nature of the work and the fundamental principles of cooperation. He can be quite vocal in his rejection of status quo theological positions with older staff members and outspoken against the existing church structures. He, like all persons entering into a cooperative ministry, needs to understand the nature of the assignment and should make a definite commitment to participation within the work.

The professional worker (usually a woman) who is assigned to a cooperative parish has a difficult place to fill. Some denominations have trained workers who are specialists in nonmetropolitan church work and are assigned by the denomination to the position, and sometimes a specialist will be assigned or elected for work in Christian education within a cooperative parish. The most frequent problems which have occurred with the professional worker are lack of a clear-cut job description, lack of understanding of lines of authority, failure to understand the fundamentals of staff relationships and how to work with others, and lack of understanding of cultural patterns of the area in which she is doing her work. Obviously there are many professional workers who have little difficulty in adjusting to staff work, but many do have problems. Frankness on the part of all persons on the staff in working through human relations will be beneficial.

The basic "distances" between members of a cooperative staff which need to be overcome are distances in age, theology, concept of the church, concept of the cooperative parish, education, cultural background, denominational background, and concepts of ethics and morality.

The alert parish director, along with the entire staff, will take time to understand differences and attempt to create situations in which differences will be minimized in favor of points of mutual concerns. Differences are not so important as long as communication is maintained and there are open minds. All persons on the staff need to develop a "listening habit" to hear the other members of the staff and to have respect for their positions. Frequent discussion, fellowship situations, parties, and informal gatherings assist greatly in coming to know the whole person rather than just the categories in which there are disagreements. One staff in the author's acquaintance, in which all of the above "distances" are present, has a Monday morning meeting on a riverbank in a sixteen-foot mobile home and finds this tremendous therapy. All staffs cannot enjoy this luxury, but they can create situations which will fulfill the same need.

All members of a cooperative staff need to have a working knowledge in the field of human relations. Time could be well spent if the staff would study together in the field. George R. Terry defines human relations:

146

"Stated succinctly, by human relations is meant the integration of the manpower resources for effective and maximum utilization by means of satisfying human wants and the maintaining of satisfactory relationships among the members seeing those human wants."[1]

Each person will bring into a parish staff a hope of being able to satisfy his own personal wants and to make a contribution to the mutual concerns of the total staff. Basically the personal wants can be summarized as (1) an opportunity for self-expression; (2) an opportunity to be recognized as an individual; (3) an opportunity to be accepted by the other members of the staff; (4) an opportunity to have a fair and equitable work load along with other members of the staff and to share a fair amount of pay and other remunerations; (5) acceptable working conditions; and (6) efficient leadership.

Those who are endowed with leadership responsibilities in a staff, such as the director, will expect from each member of the staff dependability, loyalty, creativeness, resourcefulness, cooperation, honesty, and a reasonable quantity of work well done.[2]

If a staff of a cooperative ministry is to attain the highest efficiency, each member should bring into accord with the other members his personal desires and goals of life, the desires of the leadership of the parish, and the parish objectives. Again it is stated that parish goals and objectives need to be clearly defined. As they are defined, persons on the staff will need to bring their own talents to bear upon attaining the goals. When a "we" feeling emerges in team ministry, the staff will begin to attain the proper perspective of group accomplishment.

LEADERSHIP AUTHORITY

One of the most vexing problems of staff relationships in a cooperative parish is that of authority for action and responsibility for the leader. I have encountered two major problems in cooperative parishes: either the director was elected or appointed to the position but had no authority for administrative leadership, *or* the director did not understand basic leadership principles and misused his authority, causing estrangement with other members of the staff.

Authority in the management sense, as has been defined by literature in personnel management, means power which is placed in a leader which gives him the right to initiate, act, and exact action out of others. Along with this definition is the basic concept that authority needs to be invested in a leader commensurate with his responsibility. The reverse of this is also true. In other words, when a director of a cooperative parish is elected or appointed to the position, he is automatically held responsible for action and results. He must be granted the authority to act and to lead in order that such expected results can be forthcoming. In the atmosphere of democratic action, a council of a cooperative parish or denominational executive will be afraid of granting too much authority to a director for fear he will not be fair to other members of the staff. This only leads to frustration on the part of all staff persons and inevitable failure of the cooperative enterprise. *Freedom for action comes through structured authority.* It is highly recommended that when a cooperative parish is established, involving an employed staff, a director be elected or appointed and granted enough authority to be able to initiate, act, and help each person on the staff make a full contribution to the entire enterprise. In an episcopal form of church government the appointment needs to be made by the bishop.

In some instances the leader is elected by the group for a stated period of time, and then another person is elected as leader. A "team" concept is held by the staff, and the leader becomes a convenor and moderator of staff meetings. There are problems with such an arrangement, but it may have merit provided all members of the staff are near the same age, and have equal education and leadership ability.

Misused authority is the beginning of staff decay. Leaders need to study the democratic principles of leadership and to understand the proper use of their position. Authority is automatically granted to a leader by the office he holds, but support in authority is gained by one's peers through an *earning* process. One is effective as a leader and will gain support for his leadership when he has proved personal integrity, honesty, sincerity, ability to produce in his own field, and a genuine support of the total enterprise. When any one of these qualities is missing and a doubt is forthcoming in the minds of staff members, then there is trouble ahead.

A good leader never uses the power of his office with overt authority. He is skillful in creating a situation in which group decisions are made and the abilities of staff are utilized to meet the needs of the parish. He will constantly keep in mind the personal desires of individuals on the staff and attempt to keep lines of communication open so all persons can obtain a maximum of self-fulfillment.

DENOMINATIONAL OBLIGATIONS

Every denomination has polity procedures in regard to placement of ministers. One of the most important aspects of polity is the adaptation by a denomination, or adoption by a regional governing body, of policies in regard to cooperative parishes. Three major areas of polity need to be considered: (1) qualifications of persons assigned or elected to parish staffs; (2) protection of the position in the staff when changes are made; and (3) a complete description of the position and statement of expected participation for the person being assigned to a cooperative parish. When any one of these three aspects is ignored, a foundation is laid for potential trouble. A brief discussion of the three points follows:

1. In assigning a person to a cooperative parish, care should be taken that the person has the necessary qualifications for the position. Something has been said about this earlier in this chapter. A "loner" will have difficulty working with others. Also a person who is overly dominant will have difficulties. A person who may have a negative attitude toward the church in town and country may feel he is being punished or degraded in his work. Every effort needs to be made to select persons who feel they are being challenged by the opportunity before them and that the task is one that will give ample expression to one's ministry.

2. Changes are necessary from time to time in the staff of a cooperative parish. When changes are made, the parish council or the denominational authorities need to take precaution that leadership is put into the parish which will continue with the program. A person should not be

appointed simply to "take care" of a situation, but care should be taken in the selection, with the type of leadership needed kept in mind.

3. Any person who is elected or appointed to a parish staff needs to have a complete briefing of the situation before he gets into the work. He needs to be informed of the nature of the work, lines of authority, his responsibilities, and his role in the staff. This is an area in which job descriptions are helpful. I visited in a larger parish where one minister was appointed to serve along with two other ministers. The superintendent had not explained the parish structure thoroughly and had failed to say there was a director of the parish already appointed. Naturally there are problems for the minister who comes into the parish with one idea and finds a different existing situation.

In closing this chapter, I add the thought that as long as there is human will, there will be conflicts of wills when people are engaged in a close working relationship. The task of a parish staff is to minimize conflict as much as possible by practicing democratic action, give-and-take, charity, and above all, each person must carry his share of the load of work. The parish staff which finds time to fellowship together, plan together, work together, and worship together with an understood goal and objective will most likely find individual and corporate success in their work.

CHAPTER VII

Research in Preparation
for a Cooperative Ministry

The establishment of any type of a cooperative program should be preceded by sound research and survey. One of the pitfalls of larger parishes and group ministries has been the failure of leaders to recognize the natural forces of population, social groups, topography of the land, and economic factors, as they establish parishes. Brunner, for instance, in his 1933 study of the larger parish, realized parishes must have two physical factors to survive: (1) They must be a natural sociological unit, that is, a community; and (2) they must have sufficient economic resources to support themselves in normal times. To these criteria could be added other factors such as a sufficiently large number of Protestant prospects to make the churches adequate to support a program, a spirit of cooperation between congregations and ministers, a willingness of the people to pool financial and leadership resources, the un-reserved support of the central town church, and a population which shows signs of enough stability for continued progress.

Not infrequently church leaders have plunged into a parish organization without sufficient knowledge of the ecological factors of the life of the population, only to find an organizationally impossible situation facing the parish. Time, energy, and disappointment will be saved when one does comprehensive research in preparation for the parish. Research findings when presented in graphic and tabular form will assist the people of a local area in understanding more fully their need for a cooperative undertaking by the churches.

The research does not need to be exhaustive; nor does it need to be done by a specialist. Nevertheless, if special help is available from a denominational executive, professor of sociology, or a professor of church administration, such help should be used. It is possible, in some situations, for a study to be done by a student or a group of students as a project in a college or seminary course.

The basic items for research are presented in this chapter. A detailed questionnaire to be used by the local congregations is presented in Appendix B. Additional helps are suggested in the bibliography.

DELINEATION OF NEIGHBORHOOD AND COMMUNITY

The basic essential of a closely integrated larger parish, yoked field, enlarged charge, or extended ministry, inter-denominational or denominational, is to confine the area to one community. A loosely integrated larger parish or group ministry can function efficiently if it embraces two or more rural communities provided they are part of an enlarged community. The definitions of these meaningful sociological units (as given in Chapter I) are reviewed to refresh them in the mind of the reader. "A community consists of the social interaction of people and their institutions in the local area in which they live on dispersed farmsteads and in a hamlet or village which forms the center of their common interests." "An enlarged community is two or more communities bound together in a natural or political area with a dominant town in which all communities find a common interest." A review of Chapter I will assist in understanding these basic structural units.

In establishing a closely integrated larger parish, the delineation of the community is necessary, and the boundaries of the parish should not go beyond the community. People will work together intimately in a community. They are accustomed to face-to-face relationships in school, church, trade, and social activities. They will not work closely together beyond community lines. Within a closely integrated larger parish there is one budget for several churches and two or more employed workers serving the entire parish. The parish council must serve as one board to direct the work of the parish, and the churches must have affinities sufficiently strong to override suspicion and friction. The same principle holds true for the yoked field, enlarged charge, or extended ministry.

In the loosely integrated larger parish or group ministry, each minister serves one or more congregations and derives his support from his charge. The parish council is not concerned with dispensing salaries to ministers. It assists the work of the local church but is not an "official board" in the administrative sense that it is for the closely integrated parish. Therefore, the loosely integrated parish or group ministry can cover more than one community. When it does, it should not go beyond one enlarged community. In the enlarged community there is one dominant town such as the county seat or leading trade center and two or more subdominant towns. A subdominant town is smaller in population and is able to offer fewer services than the dominant town. There are enough ties between the people of an enlarged community to warrant a loosely organized cooperative parish as they look to the dominant town for agricultural specialists, hospital service, and other professional leadership.

To delineate means to define. It can be recalled that one of the characteristics of the community is that it can be defined. It has geographic limitations. Among rural sociologists the delineation of the community has been done very effectively by determining common areas of trade and other areas of social interaction.

It was near the beginning of the century that a young sociologist accidentally discovered a method of delineating the rural trade community. Charles J. Galpin reported in 1911 on his work in Walworth County, Wisconsin:

Take the village as the community center; start out from here on any road into the open country; you come to a home, and the deep wear of the wheels out of the yard toward the village indicates that this home naturally goes to this village for trade, doctor, post office, church, lodge, entertainment, high school; the next home the same, and the next and the next, until by and by you come to a home where the ruts run the other way and grass grows a little perhaps in the turn toward this village, and you find that this home goes to an adjoining town for its major associations; between these two homes is the bounding line of the community.[1]

Thus the trade area of a central town becomes the community area according to Galpin's discovery. This discovery has been explored by many researchers since that date, and the methods of community delineation have been based upon the assumption that where people derive their primary (that is, oft-repeated) services, such as food, school, church, doctor, entertainment, they will develop a community solidarity.

There are two primary ways of determining the trade or service area of a community. The first method is the modern sequel to Galpin's observations. Most states now place on county maps the average traffic flow per twenty-four hours at stated points along highways and secondary roads. The traffic-flow meter which operates by photoelectric cell, or with a rubber hose across the highway, is a common sight to the motorist. For a nominal sum, usually not more than one dollar, a traffic-flow map for a county can be obtained from the state highway department. By finding on a given road the low point of traffic flow, it can be assumed that this is the point of division between two trade centers to which local residents go for their primary services.

Circumscribing a town, on the map one can find the low figure of traffic flow on each road. Connect these points by a line, and the trade area community is defined. Figure 9 illustrates the process, showing a section of the traffic-flow map of Ellis County, Texas. The communities and neighborhoods in Figure 1 (page 36) were delineated by the traffic-flow process.

The second method of community delineation is to reverse the process of the traffic-flow method: that is, by starting in the trade center village and working out to the extremity of the community. Page 28 lists the six services needed by all people for normal existence: economic,

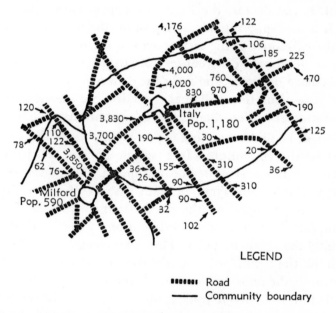

LEGEND

▪▪▪▪▪▪ Road
——— Community boundary

Source: Traffic-flow map of Ellis County, Texas, Texas Highway Department, Texas Highway Planning Survey, Austin.

Figure 9. Ellis County, Texas, traffic flow per twenty-four hour period. By finding on each highway and secondary road the point of lowest traffic flow per twenty-four hour period, it can be assumed that that point is the dividing line between communities. Connecting the points of lowest traffic flow around the town will determine the trade-area community.

educational, religious, social, communicational, and professional. By talking with the persons in the trade center town, one can secure information of how far people come for the services. Take a map of the county to the grocer and ask him to spot on the map the homes in each direction whose residents trade at his store. Do the same for the garage operator, the service station operator, the banker, the doctor, the local newspaper editor. Ask the high school superintendent to plot on the map the homes at the extremity of the service area of the school. Connect the homes for the different services, drawing a line around the village or town. The areas for each service will not be the same, but this will make a fairly well-defined configuration revealing the trade-area community.

It will be discovered that the larger the town, the larger will be the community. In a simple general science experiment there is a demonstration of the power of a magnet. With a magnet beneath a sheet of paper, iron filings are dropped on the paper. Immediately the magnetic force is seen in the configuration of the iron filings around the magnetic poles. This is an elementary illustration of the "pull" of a trade center in a community. Naturally the more services a trade center can offer and the farther it is between trade-center towns, the larger will be the community. It is a safe hypothesis that a closely integrated larger parish, yoked field, enlarged charge, or extended ministry may be established within a community delineated in the above fashion. It is possible that racial, ethnic, or class factors will enter in, which will make for a lack of harmony. These factors do not appear in delineating the community by the trade-center area.

The enlarged community consists of one dominant town and two or more subdominant towns with their surrounding rural neighborhoods. The enlarged community is delineated in a similar manner to the community. The county is used as a basis for beginning the study. Many counties across the nation are becoming "community-like" since the central town, usually the county seat, supplies all of the services needed by the individual. In such a town will be a small hospital (one or more), several lawyers, a public park, a library, and dealers in farm machinery, automobiles, and large appliances. Professional help such as an agricultural extension agent, a soil conservationist, and a home demonstration agent are in the larger town. Many central towns have the office of the regional Farm Bureau, Grange, or Farmers' Union.

A good way to start delineating an enlarged community is to take a map to the county agricultural extension agent. He will be able to point out the affinities of persons within the county and their dependence upon the central town. He can point out natural barriers such as unbridged rivers, mountains, lakes, or forests which keep people from making the central town their trade center for buying large items like farm machinery and automobiles.

Should there be two dominant towns in a county, it is quite likely that there will be two enlarged communities. Figure 1, mapping Ellis County, Texas, shows clearly two enlarged communities in the county with the central towns of Waxahachie and Ennis, respectively.

It is possible that the enlarged community might reach beyond the county line. A rural neighborhood across the county line can be dependent upon one of the subdominant towns for primary trade and associations. The political boundary is not as strong as trade ties.

With the development of the consolidated school, it has been discovered that community boundaries and the extent of influence of the enlarged community are being redrawn to conform to the consolidated school boundaries. Ties made by children and young people in their associations in school activities are very strong.

The final test of a community and enlarged community delineation is by actually asking a series of questions of residents near the edge of what the researcher thinks is the boundary of the community, based upon his preliminary study. Sometimes, to save travel time, the questionnaire is put into the hands of children and young people in school. This method is not as reliable as the actual house-to-house visit but will be sufficient to begin the work of a parish. Questions such as the following should be asked:

1. Where does the family buy groceries?
2. Where does the family go to movies?
3. Where does the family buy gasoline?
4. In case a piece of farm machinery is broken during harvest, where does one go to buy small repair parts?
5. Where does the family buy cars?
6. Where does the family go for a medical doctor?
7. Where does the family go if in need of hospitalization?
8. Where does the family go to church?
9. Where do the young people attend high school?
10. Where do the children go to elementary school?
11. Where does the family attend Farm Bureau, Grange, or Farmers' Union meetings?

12. Where does the mother in the home buy the winter wardrobe for herself and family?

Space can be left at the end of each sentence to write in the name of towns. It is possible to put the names of town into the questionnaire and simply ask the persons to check under each item.

Questions 1, 2, 3, 4, 6, 8, 10, and 11 are indicative of community relationships. These are primary services, or oft-repeated services, and are usually available at the community trade center. Questions 5, 7, 9, and 12 are guides to the enlarged community. With the exception of attendance at high school, they are services which are not needed often. Consolidation of schools in many cases has made the dominant town in an enlarged community more important.

A little practice and careful observation in community delineation will aid the novice in rural sociology to become efficient in understanding the natural groupings of the area under study.[2]

POPULATION ANALYSIS

Population is people, and people are the mission of the church. Therefore, what is happening to population is of vital importance to the church.

In an area being considered for a cooperative ministry, a thorough analysis of population should be made. The published reports of the United States Census of Population are the best information. Reports are available in public libraries, college libraries, or can be bought for a particular state for a nominal sum.[3]

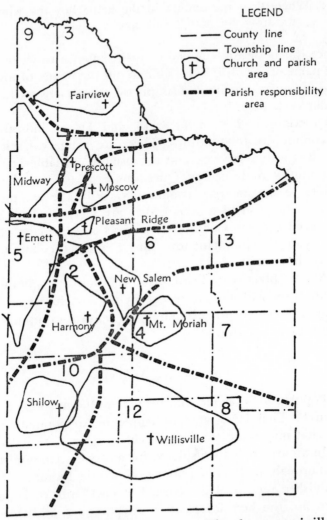

Figure 10. Nevada County, Arkansas. The above map is illustrative of four major areas of research in preparation for a cooperative parish: (1) location of all churches in the denomi-

If a more detailed report of population for a segment of a county is desired, it can be secured through a special order from the Director, Bureau of Census, Washington, D.C. 20225. Unpublished data for a township or census area, for instance, can be supplied on census enumeration areas, along with a map showing the areas. Such information will cost approximately fifteen dollars per township or census area.[4]

The trend in population for thirty to fifty years should be traced. The smallest population unit should be used, e.g., town, township, or census area. Figure 10 shows Nevada County, Arkansas, a typical rural county, with township divisions. Table 2 is typical of how trends can be reported. In this manner a very small segment of the county can be examined. By placing the churches on the map (as is done in Figure 2 for one denomination), the trends in the area of the church can be studied. A comparison of trends in church membership over a stated period of time and in population over the same period of time can reveal whether or not the church is keeping pace or losing ground.

The internal composition of population should be examined. Helpful data to be compiled are (1) white and nonwhite; (2) urban and rural farm; rural nonfarm; (3) age-sex distribution; (4) employment status; and (5) educational achievement. All of these items can be secured from published census reports. The use of the material is dependent upon the ingenuity of the leaders of the parish.

---

nation involved; (2) location of the parish area of each church; (3) parish responsibility lines; and (4) township lines and township numbers. Table 2 shows the population trend by townships.

Table 2. Population Changes by Minor Civil Divisions, 1910-1960.
NEVADA COUNTY, ARKANSAS

No.	Township Town or City	1910	1920	1930	1940	1950	1960	Change 1910-60	%Change 1910-60	Change 1950-60	%Change 1950-60
	TOTAL	19,344	21,934	20,407	19,869	14,781	10,700	− 8,644	−44.6	−4,081	−27.6
1	Alabama tp	1,139	1,116	1,125	948	687	403	− 736	−64.6	− 284	−41.3
2	Albany tp	1,464	2,194	1,752	1,467	925	492	− 972	−66.3	− 433	−46.8
3	Boughton tp	1,337	1,224	1,046	903	678	446	− 891	−66.6	− 232	−34.2
4	Caney tp	1,100	1,277	1,145	1,390	931	620	− 480	−43.6	− 311	−33.4
5	Emmet tp	867	1,182	1,007	1,020	782	633	− 234	−26.9	− 149	−18.1
	Emmet t	270	420	387	465	482	674	+ 204	+56.9	− 8	− 1.6
6	Georgia tp	833	785	675	651	408	182	− 651	−78.1	− 226	−55.3
7	Jackson tp	1,061	1,173	867	644	379	265	− 796	−75.0	− 114	−30.0
8	Leake tp	730	742	897	834	554	325	− 405	−55.4	− 229	−41.3
9	Missouri tp	4,978	5,635	5,814	6,188	5,741	4,823	− 155	− 3.1	− 918	−15.9
	Prescott c	2,705	2,691	3,033	3,177	3,960	3,533	+ 828	+23.4	− 427	−10.7
10	Parker tp	1,629	1,900	1,615	1,484	888	514	−1,115	−68.4	− 374	−42.1
11	Redland tp	1,389	1,545	1,126	1,129	775	516	− 873	−62.8	− 259	−33.4
12	Taylor tp	1,531	1,934	2,188	2,211	1,423	998	− 533	−34.8	− 425	−29.8
13	Union tp	1,286	1,227	1,150	1,000	610	483	− 803	−62.4	− 127	−20.8

Negro population: 3,857.
Source: U.S. Census of Population: 1910 to 1960.

All materials should be graphed and charted. This provides a visual way of presenting the data to individuals and groups.

ECONOMIC ANALYSIS

A stable population and a stable church are dependent upon a stable economy. Information should be secured which will give some basis of judgment as to the stability of the area under study. Sources for the study are published reports such as the Farm Census (available through the United States Department of Agriculture), business reports of the chamber of commerce, farm bureau, state universities, and utility companies. Many states have organizations composed of numerous agencies that pool resources to promote economic enterprises. Such organizations will make available their published information.

To assist further in understanding the economic condition of a region, the level of living for farm families can be secured.[5] The level of living index is based on one hundred as the average for the nation. Therefore, below one hundred or above one hundred indicates the status of the county in comparison with the national average. The index is usually based upon four items: (1) percent of farms with electricity; (2) percent of farms with telephones; (3) percent of farms with automobiles; and (4) average value of products sold or traded in the year preceding the census (adjusted for changes in the purchasing power of the farmer's dollar).

Nevada County, Arkansas, has the following level of living indexes for the years 1930, 1940, 1945, 1950, 1955, 1960, 1965: 34, 30, 37, 64, 86, 90, and 94 respectively. It will be observed that the county falls below the national average. When the recent farm statistics are observed, however, there is a clear indication that because of irrigation and raising chickens instead of cattle, the income is rising. Both the value of land and the size of farms have increased. Though population is decreasing in Nevada County, Arkansas, there is a better economic base for those who are remaining.

PARISH RESPONSIBILITY AREAS

The Protestant church has never taken seriously the geographic parish as has the Roman Catholic Church. Among Catholics definite boundaries are drawn for a local congregation. When a family moves into the parish, the church membership is automatically moved to that parish. The individual has been left the choices by Protestantism of which congregation he will join and to which congregation he will transfer his membership.

Protestants should, however, have "parish responsibility areas." That is, lines should be drawn between congregations, designating the area in which the local church is responsible for pastoral care and evangelism. Such parish boundaries do not confine the initiative of the individual but simply designate responsibility areas. In this manner no person is left outside the responsibility of a church. Many studies have revealed large sections of population outside the responsibility areas of existing congregations.

The first step in establishing responsibility areas is to discover the territories the churches are actually serving. This is done by asking the ministers to plot on a map the homes in which there are members of the local congregation. When the memberships are put together on a master map, a configuration of parish areas will take shape. Lines reaching the members on the extremity of the parish can be drawn around each church.

A more simple, though not as accurate, method of determining parish areas is to prepare a sheet containing concentric circles. In the center is located the church. In each direction from the church the pastor will draw roads. He will place a dot on each road, locating the home of the farthest resident-member from the church. These dots are connected with an irregular line around the church. The area enclosed is the territory the church is actually serving. By placing on a master map the parish area, overlapping responsibility territory can be discovered, and areas unreached by any church will be revealed. Figure 10 shows the parish areas of the Methodist churches of Nevada County, Arkansas.

THE HOUSE-TO-HOUSE CANVASS

In obtaining accurate information on church potentials, nothing exceeds the house-to-house canvass in securing data from which the religious nature of a community can be discovered. To make a house-to-house canvass over an extensive territory, however, is a very large task involving a great deal of time. If the cooperative ministry has a full-time employed staff member serving the whole area, the house-to-house canvass can be a project of that person. It is not wise to undertake a study on a wide scale with voluntary help until a cooperative parish is well under way. Sometimes in the enthusiasm of a newly organized

167

parish, someone will suggest as the first joint project of the parish a census of the whole area. This sounds good, but when faced with the reality of making such a canvass, the people find that the spirit of the parish is frequently dampened. The matter of a parish-wide, house-to-house canvass should be postponed until the parish is well organized and there is an adequate staff to give leadership to such an undertaking. Generally a parish is not ready for this type of work until it has been organized for at least two years.

When parish responsibility lines have been plotted on a map for each local church, there will usually be some part of the geographic region which is not being reached by any of the existing congregations. If this is the case, such as is found in townships 6, 11, and 13 of Nevada County, Arkansas, in Figure 10, a concentrated study can be made of such a section by all churches of the parish. A house-to-house survey should be made to determine how much church potential there is and why the residents of the area are not being reached by the existing congregations. Such a study may reveal the need for organizing another congregation. It might reveal a heavy ethnic or racial group who are members of another congregation not cooperating in the parish.

DATA ON CHURCH ORGANIZATION

To obtain a broad understanding of the church in its existing state, data should be secured concerning the ministry, church building, parsonage or manse, historical information, organizational structure, church school, and other timely information. To secure such information, a questionnaire can be placed in the hands of each minister. He should be instructed to secure the assistance of a lay committee to answer all questions. When information from each church is compiled by a central committee, or by one individual, the total church situation in a given area under study can be secured.

To assist in research on the local church, a detailed questionnaire is given in Appendix B.

Epilogue

This book should not be brought to an abrupt close with the emphasis on research. There is far more to a cooperative parish than sociological forces, maps, graphs, and statistics. There is more to a cooperative parish than careful, well-planned meetings. There is more to a cooperative parish than good leadership requirements. The larger parish is a philosophy. It will work only as long as the leaders possess the spirit of service—service to all persons within the parish by all ministers and congregations. The spirit of Christ must permeate the entire procedure, or techniques and methods simply become tools inadequate to do a task so desperately needed in the nonmetropolitan United States.

Love must be the dominant motive of all leaders—a love akin to the New Testament *agape,* a love which loves when there is little response, a love which loves when there are few material rewards, but a love which will eventually find response, bringing revival to old churches and strengthening the work of the kingdom of God.

The primary relationships of life are in the family, neighborhood, community, and church. In a day when massing of people in an impersonal society is permeating all of life, the survival of the primary group is in jeopardy as never before in history. Only can the great qualities of love, affection, and moral integrity be passed on from generation to generation in the primary group, basically, the family, neighborhood, and church. It is imperative that churchmen recognize the truth of the verse "God setteth the solitary in families" (Psalms 68:6a), and overtly perform a ministry which will keep virile the family, neighborhood, community, and church. The cooperative parish forms a framework for such ministry.

Appendix A

From the thirty-five Larger Parishes studied by Ralph A. Felton, a constitution was written which includes the main items needed to carry on such an organization. It is given here with the hope that it may be useful to groups of churches, pastors, or denominational leaders wishing to organize a Larger Parish.

THE CONSTITUTION OF THE LARGER PARISH *

ARTICLE I. NAME. The name of this organization shall be the

_____ Larger Parish.
(Name)

ARTICLE II. PURPOSE. The purpose of this Larger Parish is to minister to all the people within its area by a program of activities that can best be carried on by the cooperation of several churches.

ARTICLE III. MEMBERSHIP.

Section 1. Any church within the area may become a member of the Larger Parish when it desires by showing a willingness to do its part in all the undertakings of the parish and upon adoption of the constitution and election of representatives to the council.

* Ralph A. Felton, *The Art of Church Cooperation*, Department of Town and Country Work, The Methodist Church, New York, 1948. Used by permission.

172

Section 2. Any church may withdraw from the parish if the council has been given notice of said intention three months beforehand.

Section 3. All persons who are members of the cooperating churches also become members of the Larger Parish.

ARTICLE IV. THE LARGER PARISH COUNCIL.

Section 1. The Larger Parish Council shall be the governing body of the Larger Parish.

Section 2. The council shall be composed of four representatives from each church: the Sunday school superintendent, a young person to represent the youth, a member of the governing body of the church, and a woman to represent the women's organizations. Any other person who is a member of one of the churches may attend the meetings.

Section 3. The officers of the council shall be president, vice-president, secretary, and treasurer.

Section 4. The council shall meet every three months. One of these meetings each year shall be for the election of officers and the consideration of finances.

Section 5. All members of the staff shall be ex officio members of the council and may attend all meetings and may be elected to office.

Section 6. The council shall plan the program and activities for the parish.

ARTICLE V. THE STAFF.

Section 1. The staff shall be composed of the pastors of each of the cooperating churches, the denominational supervisors of each, the directors of religious education, the music director, and the summer workers.

Section 2. There shall be a chairman and secretary elected by the staff. The chairman shall preside or appoint someone to preside at all staff meetings. The secretary shall keep a record of all meetings.

Section 3. It shall be the work of the staff to cooperate with the council in carrying out the activities and program decided upon by the council. Each member of the staff may be assigned to various committees to help guide the activities.

ARTICLE VI. FINANCE.

Section 1. Each church shall continue its local and denominational obligations as before it became a member of the Larger Parish.

Section 2. Each church is responsible to the Larger Parish only for amounts that have been pledged by the church. But each church shall be expected to share its part of the financial affairs of the parish.

Section 3. All money for the Larger Parish shall be paid to the treasurer, who shall pay all bills upon the vote of the council.

ARTICLE VII. DENOMINATIONAL RELATIONS.

Section 1. The program of the Larger Parish shall not interfere with the denominational practice or program of any of the cooperating churches.

Section 2. Interdenominational fellowship shall be one of the goals of the Larger Parish.

ARTICLE VIII. RELATION TO OTHER ORGANIZATIONS.

Section 1. The Larger Parish shall cooperate wherever possible with all the organizations that make for community improvement.

Section 2. Special emphasis shall be placed on the importance of cooperation with the schools within the parish.

ARTICLE IX. AMENDMENTS. Amendments to this constitution shall be presented to the staff and then presented to the council. If two thirds of the members present at the council meeting vote for the amendment it shall become effective immediately.

Appendix B

To assist in research for preparation for a cooperative ministry, a questionnaire is given here. This questionnaire is one used by the author in a study of the Little Rock Conference of The Methodist Church.

When questionnaires are used, every effort should be made to secure complete and accurate data from each church involved in the study. A study is good only insofar as the information is complete.

STUDY GUIDE

_____ District

_____ Pastor

_____ Address

A. The Church in the Community.

1. Name of church_____ Charge_____.
2. P.O. Address _____ Town_____
   County _____ Township_____.
3. Number of churches on charge _____. (*A study guide should be prepared for each church on the charge.*)
4. The church is located in: open country _____; village or town _____; city _____. Population, if known _____. If a city church, it is: downtown

_____; residential _____; suburban _____; other (specify) _____.
_____

5. If church is in town of 2,500 or less, or open country, from what distance can the church be reached with good roads? _____

6. How far is the nearest church of the same denomination? _____ Blocks; _____ Miles.

7. Is the church well marked with a sign or signs?_____. A bulletin board? _____.

8. Does the charge provide a parsonage? Yes _____; No _____. How far from this church? _____ Blocks; _____ Miles

9. Where is the pastor's study located? Church _____; Parsonage _____; None _____.

10. The minister:
How many years have you served in the ministry? _____.

How many years in present charge? _____
How many charges have you served? _____.
Education: Please fill in the following table:

	YEAR ATTENDED	NAME OF SCHOOL	YEAR GRADUATED	DIPLOMA OR DEGREE
High School				
College				
Seminary				
Other				

B. History and Organization.

1. In what year was the church organized? _____.

2. Has the church ever sponsored the formation of another church? Yes _____; No _____. A church school? Yes _____; No _____; Dates _____.

3. What is the status of the sponsored group at present? Active _____; Inactive _____; Dissolved _____.

4. This committee believes that a survey to determine the need of a new church should be conducted in the area of

_____

The boundaries of this area are:

a. Northern limits. Street or highway_____.
b. Eastern limits. Street or highway_____.
c. Southern limits. Street or highway_____.
d. Western limits. Street or highway_____.

C. Building and Equipment.

1. In what year was the present building erected?_____
Date when last finished (redecorated) inside?_____
Additions were added to building in the years_____.

2. What is the general condition of the church building (s) ? Good _____; Fair _____; Major repairs needed _____; Condemned _____.

3. What is the general condition of the parsonage? Good _____; Fair _____; Major repairs needed _____. List the major repairs needed _____

_____

_____.

4. How many rooms in the parsonage? _____. Do they provide adequate living space for the minister's family? Yes _____; No _____.

5. Does the parsonage have the following equipment: central heat _____; gas heat _____; refrigeration _____; electricity _____; plumbing complete_____; plumbing partial _____; power washer _____; complete furnishings _____; air conditioning _____.

6. Are the church buildings and equipment considered adequate for the needs of the congregation? Yes _____;
No _____. Explain _____
_____.

D. Finances.

1. How much was raised for all purposes last year?_____
_____ (Amount reported in last conference journal or denominational year book.)
2. List the approximate amount of the budget raised last year from the following sources: (consult your church treasurer for accuracy.)
Contributions of members through systematic giving
$_____.
Special offerings (such as Easter, Christmas, etc.)
$_____.
Endowments $_____.
3. Is the church engaged in a special building fund campaign? Yes _____; No _____. If yes, give goal for campaign $_____; collected to date
$_____; pledged to date above collected
$_____.
4. How many members following consistent systematic giving? _____ (pay regularly to church weekly or monthly).
5. Is there an annual every-member canvass to secure pledges to underwrite the budget? Yes _____; No _____.
6. Has the church any indebtedness? Yes _____; No _____; Amount $_____.
7. For what reason was the debt assumed?_____
_____.
8. How long has it been carried?_____. How is it being taken care of?_____.
9. If financial aid is received from outside the church, list

where: Conference or association board of missions
_____; Sustentation or minimum salary fund
_____; General board of missions_____.
Amount in current year $_____. How many
years has there been such aid? _____.

E. *Membership.*

1. Number of church members reported in last conference
   journal or year book _____.
2. Number of church members who do not live in the immediate vicinity of the church. These might be called
   nonresident members _____.
3. Number of people listed on the constituency roll or
   prospect roll _____.
4. What is the average attendance at Sunday morning
   church worship service for the past six months?_____.
   Evening service _____.
5. During the past five years, how many young people from
   this church have entered the ministry or mission field?
   _____.

F. *Program and Organization.*

1. Organizations: fill in the following listings:

	NUMBER OF GROUPS	MEMBERSHIP	NUMBER OF MEETINGS PER YEAR
Women's Organization			
Men's Organization			
Youth Organization			

2. Check if committees are organized and functioning in the following areas:

	Organized	Functioning
Evangelism	Yes__; No__	Yes__; No__
Education	Yes__; No__	Yes__; No__
Missions	Yes__; No__	Yes__; No__
Christian Social Concerns	Yes__; No__	Yes__; No__
Finance	Yes__; No__	Yes__; No__
Worship	Yes__; No__	Yes__; No__

3. Does the church practice the rotation system in the official board or other governing body? Yes__; No__.

4. Activities: fill in the following inventory:

	Yes	No
Public worship every Sunday morning		
Public worship every Sunday night		
Services two Sunday mornings per month		
Services one Sunday per month		
Regular midweek service		
Special evangelistic services held last year		
Special Holy Week observance		
Daily vacation church school in last year		
Weekday religious education for children		
Mission study classes held		
Church membership preparation classes		

	Yes	No
Envelopes used weekly or monthly for offering		
Regularly adopted church budget		
Permanent membership record		
Alphabetical membership record		
Evangelistic visitation teams		
Lord's Acre program		
Regular choir (4 or more voices)		
Children's choir		
Delegates to youth camp		
Clinic or dispensary		
Supervised playground or gym		
Monthly family nights		
Weekly church bulletin (enclose a copy)		
Weekly or monthly church paper (enclose a copy)		
Regular radio program		
Regular television program		
Regular newspaper space bought		
Sponsor Boy Scouts		

	Yes	No
Sponsor Girl Scouts		
Part of group ministry		
Church is member of interdenominational council, either city or county		

List here the preaching schedule if above does not apply

_____ .

CHECK HYMNBOOK USED:	SUNDAY SCHOOL	CHURCH
Official denominational hymnal		
Other (write in name)		

(TO BE PREPARED BY CHURCHES LOCATED IN COMMUNITIES OF *2,500* POPULATION AND LESS, IN-CLUDING *OPEN* COUNTRY)

G. *The Church and Its Surroundings.*

1. How many (more or less) businesses are there in your town now than ten years ago? More_____; Less_____. (Inquire of long-time residents.)
2. What has been the (increase or decrease) in public school enrollment in the past ten years? Increase_____; Decrease_____.
3. Check the following considering the *majority* of people in the community:

	Town	Distance
Where do they buy groceries?		
Where do they buy cars?		
Where do they bank?		
Where do children attend high school?		
Where do children attend elementary school?		
Where can a doctor be secured?		
Where do they go for hospital service?		

4. Check the following if a community problem:

__Commercial recreation   __Lack opportunities for youth
__Poverty or unemployment__Lack community pride
__Poor roads   __Underchurched
__Juvenile delinquency   __Overchurched
__Inadequate leadership   __Poor public schools
                                            __Community conflict

5. Number of church members with residence in community who commute daily outside community for employment _____.

6. Is there a general migration of young people out of the community? Yes _____; No _____. Explain _____
_____.

7. Is there any type of community coordinating organization made up of various religious and secular organizations? Yes _____; No _____. If yes, does this church belong to it? Yes _____; No _____.

(TO BE PREPARED BY ALL CHURCHES)

MAP *(locating church, churches of other denominations, abandoned churches, towns)*

On this page sketch a map of the territory around the church of this questionnaire for a distance of five miles in each direction. Locate the following items on the map:

1. Major highways or streets. (Name and number them.)
2. Other churches of same denomination in the area. (Name them on map.)
3. Churches of other denominations (Names).

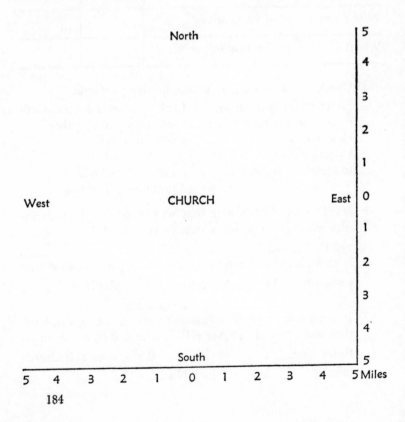

4. Abandoned churches of same denomination. (Name them.)
5. If a country church, name and locate towns in area.

INSTRUCTIONS:

Each circle represents one-half mile radius from the church.
1. Locate the church at the center of the circle at intersection of North-South and East-West lines.
2. Draw lines representing streets or roads leading from church.
3. Place a dot at the location of each church family living on each road.
4. Connect the dots at farthest extremity, drawing a line around the circles. This is an outline of the parish boundary.

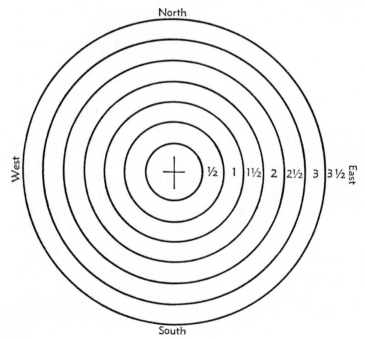

185

Appendix C

PARISH DEVELOPMENT AIDS

A six-session course designed to assist laymen and pastors in understanding the basic factors in developing, organizing, and putting into operation a cooperative parish.

Text for the course: *The Cooperative Parish in Nonmetropolitan Areas*. Additional reading: At the end of the book beginning on page 197 a bibliography makes suggestions for additional reading for each chapter in the book.

PRELIMINARY PREPARATION

The leader of the class will need to make the following preparation prior to the first session.

1. A good map of the area to be considered for a cooperative parish should be secured. State highway maps for the county either one-half inch or one inch scale are excellent maps for this purpose. They can be secured at a nominal fee.

2. A traffic-flow map should be secured for the county or counties involved. The map can be secured from the state highway department.

3. A questionnaire needs to be prepared for each church to be involved in the cooperative parish. See Appendix B for a sample questionnaire.

4. All persons should read the text before the first class session.

5. Chapter VII needs to be carefully studied and thoroughly followed.

Objective: To discover through analysis and discussion the needs of the church within the region under study.

Reports need to be made of studies that have been done, the material reported on the questionnaires, and the basic geographical features of the area under study. Some areas of discussion may be:

1. What is the general trend of churches in the area in regard to membership, church school enrollment, church school attendance?

2. How many cooperating churches are there in the area? Where are they located? What other churches of different denominations are there? What are their strengths? What churches of different racial or ethnic groups are there? What are their strengths?

3. Where are the members of the churches in the area living? What is the parish area of each church? (The parish areas need to be plotted on a map as described in Chapter VII, Figure 10.)

4. What are the charge arrangements in the area? Where do the ministers live? (Plot this information on the map.)

5. What can be discovered about the individual churches: (a) membership; (b) church school enrollment; (c) church school average attendance; (d) budgets; (e) organizations— women's and men's groups, youth groups, denominational organizations such as committees or commissions, official boards; (f) worship schedules; (g) buildings? What are the trends over the past twenty years in the above items?

6. Who are the ministers of the area? What are their pastoral responsibilities?

SESSION II: DISCOVERING NATURAL SOCIOLOGICAL AREAS

Objective: To assist persons to understand in general the nature of nonmetropolitan society and the trends affecting the church in nonmetropolitan areas, and specifically the nature of the sociological structure of the geographic area under study. The text, Chapters I and II, need to be thoroughly mastered.

In preparation for Session Two a large map of the region should be prepared which will have on it the information discovered in Session One. On the map can be outlined the locality groups I, II, and III as defined by the traffic-flow map and questionnaires.

Some areas for discussion are:

1. What are the locality groups II (rural communities) as defined by study of the area through questionnaires and traffic-flow maps? (See Chapters II and VII.)

2. Where are the rural neighborhood congregations? (Locality group I.)

3. To what communities do the rural neighborhood churches belong?

4. Are the pastoral charges arranged so as to take advantage of most logical sociological forces in the area?

5. Population analysis:
   a) Define the population census areas or townships.
   b) Trace by minor civil divisions (census areas, townships, towns, and cities) the trend in population over a period of fifty years.
   c) What ethnic and/or racial groups are there?
   d) What is the age-sex distribution? Fertility ratio?
   e) What is the rural farm, rural nonfarm, and urban population?

6. Economic analysis:
   a) How do the majority of the people make a living?

188

   b) What are the land ownership patterns? What is the farm rental pattern?

   c) What are the major industries of the region?

   d) Are there changing economic patterns in the area?

   e) Are there job opportunities for young people who want to begin their careers?

7. What effect do the forces mentioned above have on the churches in the region?

SESSION III: DEFINITIONS OF COOPERATIVE PARISHES

Objective: To assist persons to understand types of cooperative parishes, the philosophy undergirding them, and to explore what type of parish structure may be applicable for the area under study. Text: Chapter III.

Some areas of consideration may be:

1. Define the consolidated or merged church, the yoked field, the extended ministry, the larger parish, the group ministry, and the federated church. What are the differences?

2. What were the motivating forces behind Harlow S. Mills in his concept of the larger parish?

3. What were the five basic convictions of Mills regarding the work of the larger parish, and how are they applied in modern church administration?

4. Summarize the nine areas of findings regarding the larger parish as described by Edmund deS. Brunner. How are they applicable today?

5. What basic difference did Aaron Rapking make between the larger parish and group ministry?

6. While examining the map of the region, charge arrangements, congregations, and needs for the church in the region, what type or types of cooperative parishes will be the most effective?

SESSION IV: ESTABLISHING COOPERATIVE PARISHES

Objectives: To understand the process by which persons are incorporated into planning for the beginning of a cooperative parish. Text: Chapter IV.

1. What is meant by a "construct of social action"?

2. In the light of the discussion in Chapter IV define the following and apply the definition to the geographic area being studied: (1) social system boundary; (2) convergence of interests; (3) prior social situation; (4) professionals living in the system; (5) professionals outside the system; (6) the problem situation; (7) relevant social systems; (8) the initiating set; (9) legitimation; (10) diffusion set; (11) goals; (12) evaluation.

3. Who is responsible for stimulating interest in the cooperative parish?

4. Is further research needed for the cooperative parish? If so, what information needs to be obtained? Who can be of assistance in getting and interpreting the information?

5. Define clearly the basic goals and objectives of the cooperative parish.

6. How can a large number of persons be brought into planning for the cooperative parish?

7. Will there be a need for a constitution? If so, who is given responsibility for it, and what should it contain?

8. Is there a need to set up a series of meetings leading up to the final adoption of a plan to begin the cooperative parish? If so, define the nature of the meetings, programs, delegations, and tentative dates.

9. What relationships do the denominational regional representatives have to the planning process, and how are they involved?

SESSION V: THE COOPERATIVE PARISH AT WORK

Objective: To gain a clear understanding of how a cooperative parish functions. Text: Chapter V.

1. Relate the goals and objectives discussed in the previous

session to the program of the cooperative parish. A program is designed to implement the goals and objectives.

2. How is a council in a cooperative parish selected? Define the council's responsibilities.

3. List some possible areas in which a cooperative parish can work with simultaneous action in the various congregations. What advantages can there be in such action?

4. Describe a parish paper. What should its subject matter be? Who should edit such a paper? How should it be financed? How and to whom should it be circulated?

5. What is a "parish day"? Consider some of its values.

6. What type of budget should there be for a cooperative parish? How is it determined? How do the congregations share in the raising of the budget?

7. What types of committees are needed in the cooperative parish?

8. With what areas of community service should the cooperative parish be concerned, and how should the parish as such work in such enterprises.

SESSION VI: LEADERSHIP

Objective: To consider the various leadership roles in a cooperative parish and their relationships. Text: Chapter VI.

Some areas for consideration:

1. State the various leadership roles in a cooperative parish such as parish director and official board of each local church.

2. Define the responsibilities of each person or group which has leadership responsibilities.

3. What are some of the fundamental principles of good personnel management?

4. What is a job description? How does it apply to a parish staff?

5. List some of the problems which are likely to appear

among leaders in a cooperative parish and how can they be solved?

6. What is the place and function of denominational regional executives, such as a district superintendent, to the leadership of a cooperative parish?

7. What is the relationship between the parish council and the official board of each local church?

8. List some of the qualifications which a parish director needs to have to equip him for his position.

9. Discuss the types of staff meetings which need to be held by the staff of a cooperative parish. What is the philosophy behind each type of meeting?

10. What needs to be done on a denominational level to insure the continuance of a cooperative parish over a long period of time?

Notes

CHAPTER I

[1] For a full discussion see Ch. 4, "Patterns of Land Settlement," Lowry Nelson, *Rural Sociology* (New York: American Book Company, 1955); and Ch. 7, "Settlement Patterns," Charles P. Loomis and J. Allen Beegle, *Rural Social Systems* (Englewood Cliffs, N.J.: Prentice-Hall, 1950).

[2] *Rural Social Systems*, p. 187.

[3] Lawrence M. Hepple, "Implications of the Missouri Rural Church Study for the Town and Country Movement," *New Horizons for Town and Country Churches* (published by the Department of Town and Country Work, National Council of Churches of Christ in the U.S.A., 1956), p. 49. Dr. Hepple's study is reported in Research Bulletins 633A to 633G, College of Agriculture, University of Missouri, Agricultural Experiment Station, Columbia, Missouri.

[4] John H. Kolb, *Emerging Rural Communities: Group Relations in Rural Society, A Review of Wisconsin Research in Action* (Madison: The University of Wisconsin Press, 1959), p. 42. Reprinted with permission of the copyright owners, The Regents of the University of Wisconsin.

[5] *Ibid.,* p. 66.

[6] R. M. MacIver, *Community: A Sociological Study* (New York: The Macmillan Company, 1928), p. 22.

[7] Kenyon L. Butterfield, *Mobilizing the Rural Community,* Extension Bulletin No. 23 (Massachusetts Agricultural College, 1918), p. 9.

[8] Dwight Sanderson, *Locating the Rural Community,* Cornell reading course for the farm (N.W. State College of Agriculture, 1920), Lesson 158, p. 417.

[9] Dwight Sanderson, *The Rural Community: The Natural History of a Sociological Group* (Boston: Ginn and Company, 1932), p. 481.

[10] J. H. Kolb and Edmund deS. Brunner, *A Study of Rural Society* (4th ed.; Boston: Houghton Mifflin Company, 1952), p. 233.

[11] Karl A. Fox and T. Krishna Kumar, "The Functional Economic Area: Delineation and Implications for Economic Analysis and Policy" (Ames, Iowa: Iowa State University, Department of Economics, March 20, 1965), p. 13. (Mimeographed.)

[12] Charles J. Galpin, "The Social Anatomy of an Agricultural Community." Research Bulletin No. 34, Agricultural Experiment Station of the University of Wisconsin, May, 1915.

[13] Charles P. Loomis and Zona K. Loomis, *Modern Social Theories* (Princeton, N.J.: D. Van Nostrand Co., 1961), p. 3.

[14] For a detailed discussion of *community* see the bibliography at the end of the book and especially Roland L. Warren, *The Community in America* (Skokie, Ill.: Rand McNally & Co., 1963). Warren uses the social system concept as a frame of reference for community structure.

CHAPTER II

[1] The reader is directed for further detail on the subject of rural and urban differences to the following works: Sorokin and Zimmerman, *Principles of Rural-Urban Sociology* (New York: Henry Holt & Co., 1929); Ferdinand Tonnies, *Fundamental Concepts of Sociology* (New York: American Book Company, 1940); L. H. Bailey, *The Holy Earth* (New York: Charles Scribner's Sons, 1915); Rockwell C. Smith, *The Church in Our Town* (Nashville: Abingdon Press, 1955), Ch. 1; Rockwell C. Smith, *Rural Church Administration* (Nashville: Abingdon Press, 1953), Ch. 1. See also list of books on rural sociology in the bibliography at the end of this book.

[2] Adapted from Donald J. Bogue and Calvin L. Beale, "Recent Population Trends in the United States and Their Causes," in *Our Changing Rural Society; Perspective and Trends,* James H. Copp, ed. (Ames, Iowa: Iowa State University Press, 1964), p. 72.

[3] *Agricultural Statistics,* 1965 (Washington: U.S. Department of Agriculture, U.S. Government Printing Office, 1965), p. 443, Table 646.

[4] *Our Changing Rural Society,* p. 82.

[5] Willard W. Cochrane, *The City Man's Guide to the Farm Problem* (Minneapolis: University of Minnesota Press, 1965), p. 70.

CHAPTER III

[1] Harlow S. Mills, *The Making of a Country Parish* (New York: Missionary Education Movement of the United States and Canada, 1914), pp. 13, 15, 18, 20.

[2] (New York: The Institute of Social and Religious Research, 1934).

[3] *Ibid.,* p. 67.

[4] (Ithaca, N.Y.: Cornell University Extension Bulletin No. 408, 1939).

[5] *Ibid.,* p. 4.

[6] Aaron H. Rapking, "Pioneering in the Kingdom of God" (unpublished), Ch. 7. Used by permission.

[7] Douglas W. Johnson, *A Study of Methodist Group Ministries and Larger Parishes in the Inner City* (Chicago: Chicago Home Missionary and Church Extension Society, Rock River Conference of The Methodist Church, 1966).

CHAPTER IV

[1] Adapted from George M. Beal, Ross C. Blount, Ronald C. Powers, and W. John Johnson, *Social Action and Interaction in Program Planning* (Ames, Iowa: Iowa State University Press, 1966), p. 6.

[2] A detailed account can be found in *Information Service,* National Council of Churches of Christ in America, 475 Riverside Drive, New York, New York 10027, Vol. XLIV, No. 1. The article is by Horace S. Sills and is entitled "The Schellsburg Story, a Process of Ecumenical Action."

CHAPTER V

[1] Two excellent pieces of literature are *Family Farm-Operating Agreements* (East Lansing, Mich.: Michigan State University, Agricultural Experiment Station, North Central Regional Publication No. 143) and *Planning Farm Property Transfers* (Ames, Iowa: Iowa State University, 1966), bulletin P-125 (revised).

[2] *The Making of a Country Parish,* pp. 13, 15, 18, 20.

CHAPTER VI

[1] George R. Terry, *Principles of Human Management* (Homewood, Ill.: Richard D. Irwin, 1956), p. 342.

[2] *Ibid.,* p. 345.

CHAPTER VII

[1] Charles J. Galpin, *First Wisconsin Country Life Conference* (Madison, Wisc.: University of Wisconsin, the College of Agriculture, 1911), p. 12.

[2] An excellent base map for a county can be secured from the state highway department. When ordering, state the county and size. Most highway departments have "full-size" (one inch to the mile), "half-size" (one-half inch), and "one-quarter size" (one-quarter inch). Such maps list all roads, schools, churches, cemeteries, rivers, business houses, or towns and residences.

[3] Order, naming state, U.S. Census of Population: Number of Inhabitants and U.S. Census of Population: General Characteristics. Order from Superintendent of Documents, Washington, D.C. 20225. Cost for most states will not be more than $1.00.

[4] Write to the Director of Census, Washington, D.C. 20225, stating exact information desired for the exact area, and a statement will be submitted showing whether or not such information is available and what the cost will be.

[5] *Farm-Operator Family Level-of-Living Indexes for Counties of the United States,* U.S.D.A., Agricultural Marketing Service, Washington, D.C. 20225.

Bibliography

CHAPTERS I AND II

Chermayeff, Serge and Christopher Alexander. *Community and Privacy*. Garden City, N.Y.: Doubleday & Company, 1963.

Cochrane, Willard W. *The City Man's Guide to the Farm Problem*. Minneapolis: University of Minnesota Press, 1965.

Copp, James H., ed. *Our Changing Rural Society: Perspectives and Trends*. Ames, Iowa: Iowa State University Press, 1964.

Freedman, Ronald, ed. *Population: The Vital Revolution*. Garden City, N.Y.: Doubleday & Company, 1964.

Hoiberg, Otto G. *Exploring the Small Community*. Lincoln: University of Nebraska Press, 1955.

Kolb, John H. *Emerging Rural Communities*. Madison: University of Wisconsin Press, 1959.

Kolb, J. H. and Edmund deS. Brunner. *A Study of Rural Society*. 4th ed. Boston: Houghton Mifflin Company, 1952.

Landis, Paul H. *Rural Life in Process*. New York: McGraw-Hill Book Company, 1940.

Loomis, Charles P. and J. Allen Beegle. *Rural Social Systems*. Englewood Cliffs, N.J.: Prentice-Hall, 1950.

Nelson, Lowry. *Rural Sociology*. New York: American Book Company, 1955.

Nisbet, Robert A. *The Quest for Community.* New York: Oxford University Press, 1953.

Nesius, Ernest J. *The Rural Society in Transition.* Morgantown, W. Va.: Office of Research and Development of the West Virginia Center for Appalachian Studies and Development, West Virginia University. Public Affairs Series, No. 3, April, 1966. (Monograph.)

Sanders, Irwin T. *Making Good Communities Better.* Lexington: University of Kentucky Press, 1959.

————. *The Community.* 2nd ed. New York: The Ronald Press Company, 1966.

Taylor, Lee and Arthur R. Jones, Jr. *Rural Life and Urbanized Society.* New York: Oxford University Press, 1964.

Tonnies, Ferdinand. *Fundamental Concepts of Sociology (Gemeinschaft und Gesellschaft).* Tr. by Charles P. Loomis. New York: American Book Company, 1940.

Vidich, Arthur J. and Joseph Bensman. *Small Town in Mass Society.* Garden City, N.Y.: Doubleday & Company, 1960.

Vidich, Arthur J., Joseph Bensman, and Maurice R. Stein. *Reflections on Community Studies.* New York: John Wiley & Sons, 1964.

Warren, Roland L. *The Community in America.* Skokie, Ill.: Rand McNally & Co., 1963.

————, ed. *Perspectives on the American Community.* Skokie, Ill.: Rand McNally & Co., 1966.

CHAPTERS III, IV, AND V

Biddle, William W. and Loureide J. Biddle. *The Community Development Process—The Rediscovery of Local Initiative.* New York: Holt, Rinehart & Winston, 1965.

Brunner, Edmund deS. *The Larger Parish, a Movement or*

an Enthusiasm? New York: The Institute of Social and Religious Research, 1934.

Carr, James M. *Working Together in the Larger Parish.* Atlanta: The Church and Community Press, 1960.

Clark, Carl A. *Rural Churches in Transition.* Nashville: Broadman Press, 1959.

Family Farm-Operating Agreements. East Lansing, Mich.: Michigan State University. North Central Regional Publication 143.

Felton, Ralph A. *The Art of Church Cooperation.* Madison, N.J.: Drew Theological Seminary, 1948.

Fry, John R., ed. *The Church and Community Organization.* Published for the Division of Christian Life and Mission, National Council of the Churches of Christ in the U.S.A. by the Department of Publication Services, 1965.

Greene, Shirley E. *Ferment on the Fringe.* Philadelphia: The Christian Education Press, 1960.

Growing and Declining Villages in Wisconsin, 1950–1960. Madison, Wisc.: University of Wisconsin, College of Agriculture. No. 8 Population Series.

Identifying the Community Power Structure. Ames, Iowa: Iowa State University of Science and Technology, 1965. Soc. 18.

Kelley, Arleon, ed. *Ecumenical Design: Imperatives for Action in Nonmetropolitan America.* New York: National Consultation on Church in Community Life (475 Riverside Drive, New York, New York 10027), 1967.

Lindgren, Alvin L. *Foundations for Purposeful Church Administration.* Nashville: Abingdon Press, 1965.

McSwain, Harold W. *The Cooperative-Type Ministry and Renewal in Town and Country Churches.* Atlanta, Ga.: Religious Research Center, Candler School of Theology, Emory University, 1965.

Mills, Harlow S. *The Making of a Country Parish*. New York: Missionary Education Movement of the United States and Canada, 1914.

Morris, John, ed. *New Ways with the Ministry*. London: The Faith Press, 1960.

Mueller, E. W. and Giles C. Ekola. *Mission in American Outdoors*. St. Louis: Concordia Publishing House, 1966.

Mueller, E. W. and Giles C. Ekola, eds. *The Silent Struggle for Mid-America, the Church in Town and Country Today*. Minneapolis: Augsburg Publishing House, 1963.

New Thousands in Town and Country, The Church's Concern for Communities with a Rural Nonfarm Population in the Northeast U.S.A. Report of a workshop held at Gettysburg College, Gettysburg, Pennsylvania. Published by Church in Town and Country, National Lutheran Council, 327 South LaSalle Street, Chicago, Illinois, 1962.

Parish Zone System. Produced by the Division of Stewardship, the Anglican Church of Canada, 600 Jarvis Street, Toronto 5, Canada. Canon G. H. Tucker, Supervisor (foreword), 1965.

Paton, David M., ed. *The Parish Communion Today*. London: S.P.C.K., 1962.

———. *New Forms of Ministry*. I.M.C. Research Pamphlet No. 12. London: Edinburgh House Press (2 Eaton Gate, London, SWI), 1965.

Pepper, Clayton A. *Work Together As One—Federated Churches*. Valley Forge, Penn.: American Baptist Home Mission Society, 1962.

Planning Farm Property Transfers. Ames, Iowa: Iowa State University, 1966. Bulletin P-125 (revised).

Randolph, H. S. and Alice Maloney. *A Manual for Town and Country Churches*. New York: Department of the

Rural Church of the Board of National Missions, the Presbyterian Church, U.S.A., 1950.

Rapking, Aaron. *The Group Ministry.* New York: Division of Home Missions and Church Extension of The Methodist Church, n.d.

Rich, Mark: *The Larger Parish, an Effective Organization for Rural Churches.* Ithaca, N.Y.: Cornell University Extension Bulletin No. 408, 1939.

————. *The Rural Church Movement.* Columbia, Mo.: Juniper Knoll Press, 1957.

Schaller, Lyle E. *Community Organization: Conflict and Reconciliation.* Nashville: Abingdon Press, 1966.

————. *The Churches' War on Poverty.* Nashville: Abingdon Press, 1967.

Schnucker, Calvin. *How to Plan the Rural Church Program.* Philadelphia: The Westminster Press, 1954.

Settle, Lester M. *The Ministry of the Church to Rural Communities.* Masstown, Nova Scotia: Lester M. Settle, with assistance from the Joint Committee on the Rural Church, the United Church of Canada, Toronto, Ontario, 1965. (Mimeographed.)

Sills, Horace S., ed. *Grassroots Ecumenicity.* Philadelphia: United Church Press, 1967.

Smelser, Neil J., ed. *Sociology: An Introduction.* New York: John Wiley & Sons, 1967.

Smith, Arthur C. *Team and Group Ministry.* Church Information Office, Church House, Westminster, SW1, England, 1965.

Smith, Rockwell C. *The Church in Our Town.* Nashville: Abingdon Press, 1955.

————. *Rural Church Administration.* Nashville: Abingdon Press, 1953.

THE COOPERATIVE PARISH IN NONMETROPOLITAN AREAS

Webber, George W. *The Congregation in Mission.* New York: Abingdon Press, 1964.

Williamson, Ralph L. *Federated Churches.* Ithaca, N.Y.: Cornell University, Rural Church Institute.

Wilson, Robert L. and James H. Davis. *The Church in the Racially Changing Community.* Nashville: Abingdon Press, 1966.

CHAPTER VI

Beal, George M. *et al. Social Action and Interaction in Program Planning.* Ames, Iowa: Iowa State University Press, 1966.

Biddle, William W. *The Cultivation of Community Leaders.* New York: Harper & Brothers, 1953.

Bulletins on leadership and group action from Iowa State University of Science and Technology, Ames, Iowa.
Leadership. Soc. 1. 1962.
Communication. Soc. 2. 1962.
Group Member Roles. Soc. 3. 1962.
The Leader and the Group. Soc. 4. 1962.
Mister Chairman, A Booklet of Parliamentary Procedure. Soc. 10. 1963.

Knowles, Malcolm and Hulda. *Introduction to Group Dynamics.* New York: Association Press, 1959.

Gouldner, Alvin W., ed. *Studies in Leadership.* New York: Russell & Russell Publishers, 1965.

Haiman, Franklin S. *Group Leadership and Democratic Action.* Boston: Houghton Mifflin Company, 1951.

Hepple, Lawrence M. *Group Organization and Leadership in Rural Life.* Columbia, Mo.: Lucas Brothers, Publishers, 1956.

202

Poston, Waverly. *Democracy Is You.* New York: Harper & Brothers, 1953.

CHAPTER VII

The Community Survey. Ames, Iowa: Iowa State University of Science and Technology, 1964. Soc. 15.

Norton, Perry L. *Search.* National Council of Churches, 475 Riverside Drive, New York, New York 10027. 1960.

————. *The Relevant Church.* National Council of Churches, 475 Riverside Drive, New York, New York 10027. 1960.

Stotts, Herbert E. *The Church Inventory Handbook.* Denver: Wesley Press, 1951.

Young, Pauline V. *Scientific Social Surveys and Research.* Englewood Cliffs, N.J.: Prentice-Hall, 1956.

In addition to the above publications most major denominations have developed self-inventory guides for the local church. Write the denominational headquarters.

FILMS

None Goes His Way Alone. 16 mm sound, black and white or color. A story of the Johnson County, Missouri, group ministry.

Working Together. 35 mm color filmstrip with sound recording. A description of four group ministries in the United States.

Both films are available at all bookstores of The Methodist Church.

The Great Adventure: Parish Development in the Emerging Town and Country Society. 35 mm color filmstrip and recording presenting ideas for church development. National Lutheran Council, 327 South LaSalle Street, Chicago, Illinois 60604.

PERIODICALS

Rural Sociology. Journal of the Rural Sociological Society. South Dakota State University, Brookings, South Dakota 57006.

Sociologia Ruralis. Journal of the European Society for Rural Sociology. Royal Van Gorcum Ltd. (Dr. H. J. Prakke & H. M. G. Prakke.) Assen—The Netherlands.

Town and Country Church. National Council of Churches of Christ in America, 475 Riverside Drive, New York, New York 10027.

Index

205